THE HUMAN DESIGN

REFLECTOR
BAROMETER OF THE WORLD

Amber Clements

Copyright © 2021 by Amber Clements

The Human Design Reflector
Barometer of the World

All rights reserved.
No part of this work may be used or reproduced, transmitted, stored, or used in any form or by any means graphic, electronic, or mechanical, including but not limited to photocopying, recording, scanning, digitizing, taping, Web distribution, information networks, or information storage and retrieval systems, or in any manner whatsoever without prior written permission from the publisher.

Disclaimer: This book's intended purpose is not to substitute the medical advice of a physician or qualified therapist. The reader should regularly consult a physician in matters relating to his/her health and particularly with respect to any symptoms that may require diagnosis or medical attention.

An Imprint for GracePoint Publishing (www.GracePointPublishing.com).

GracePoint Matrix, LLC
624 S. Cascade Ave. #201
Colorado Springs, CO, 80903
www.GracePointMatrix.com
Email: Admin@GracePointMatrix.com
SAN # 991-6032

Library of Congress Control Number: 2020924799
ISBN-13: (Paperback)# 978-1-951694-34-0
eISBN: (eBook) # 978-1-951694-33-3

Books may be purchased for educational, business, or sales promotional use.
For bulk order requests and price schedule contact:
Orders@GracePointPublishing.com

Printed in the United States of America

For more great books, please visit
HumanDesignPress.com

Contents

PREFACE

I'VE STARTED MANY BOOKS. Often without the energy or compulsion to finish them. I thought this was due to my inability to stay focused and actually commit to something. Then I discovered human design. I say discovered because that's what finding out about being a human design Reflector type felt like; a huge discovery and unveiling of my real, naked self.

Awakening to the realisation that I was a unique energetic being who had spent the previous 40 years trying to be like everyone else, was a true revelation for me. In that moment, I was transformed.

Diving deep into my human design journey as a natural investigator and a thirsty learner, I gained a whole new perspective about life and about myself. I could no longer return to the old me. I was forever changed.

As a Reflector who spent most of her life acting like a Manifestor and a Generator type pushing through life as a high achiever, I finally understood why these achievements were satisfying but not fulfilling. I learned why I often felt disappointed because I was competent and highly capable of so many things, but I was unable to energetically sustain them.

I spent many years wondering what was wrong with me. I judged myself, fiercely comparing myself to others. My complete openness made me profusely aware of other people's judgement of me too. I felt their critique of me for not being energetically sustainable the way they were and for needing to change things up so frequently. I often didn't live up to my own high expectations and I looked everywhere externally to blame as the source of this disappointment.

Once I discovered human design, I breathed a sigh of relief. I began to love myself for all that I am and all that I'm not and started treating myself with a kindness I'd never given myself before.

Embarking on my journey of self-discovery was challenging at first. In pursuit of learning about Reflectors, I struggled to find approachable, articulate Reflector mentors who could provide me with support and guidance on my Reflector journey. I had to make sense of things through my own lived experiences as a Reflector having learned many of these things the hard way.

As a naturally inquisitive investigator, I realised that if it was a struggle for me to find solid information about being a Reflector then there must be plenty of other Reflectors feeling equally as challenged. This compelled me to write this book. I felt called to share what I've learned so far to help Reflectors on their own journey of self-discovery; to help them learn how to live a happy and healthy life as a Reflector.

After working with many Reflectors through my coaching business, I realised that many experienced similar challenges. Most Reflectors are acutely aware of their points of difference from other people and this awareness is present for most of their lives. Despite this, they manage to navigate themselves through the world as best they can, trying to fit in, trying to be like everyone else.

Most Reflectors are reasonably successful at assimilating during the first half of their lives. In the second half, around 40 years of age, the impact of assimilation starts to take a toll on their health and wellbeing. This is when they become much more susceptible to exhaustion. When Reflectors learn how to use their energy correctly, they can prepare for this and understand how to effectively work with their design to enable a fulfilling and healthy life as a Reflector.

My youthful ability to borrow energy allowed me to study teaching and communication at university, to travel, and to pursue other wonderful endeavours that gave me a strong and successful career as a teacher, an educator, and a transformation consultant and coach. I'm grateful for the career and life experiences I had in the first half of my life. They helped me hone my skills as both a writer and a teacher which I frequently draw on now as a 40-something Reflector who can no longer sustain working like I once did.

My Reflector journey of discovery never ends; every day there is something new to learn and discover about myself and the world around me. When Reflectors can do this in a healthy and sustainable way, we can walk confidently and contently in our Reflector shoes and play our part in a world that needs us now more than ever. If I can make this process any easier to navigate or provide even the smallest amount of assistance to other Reflectors and those who love them, my pursuit will be absolutely worth it. Through this book, I strive to help you too on this journey.

INTRODUCTION

REFLECTORS ARE THE RAREST of all the Human Design types. They make up only 1% of the population. That's why they're so rare to find and why it's so hard to source great information about this Human Design type.

Reflectors are still an anomaly and a mystery to many people. Many Reflectors are often confused and daunted about their Human Design type and the unique aspects of their chart can be seriously burdensome. A Reflector's overwhelming decision-making strategy and lack of sustainable energy can be hard to reckon with. When they first learn about their unusual design, many Reflectors are already detrimentally impacted by life conditioning and the world around them through all their open energy centres.

Reflectors reflect back to the world the energy of the people around them like a mirror. When you meet a Reflector, you won't necessarily see them, you'll see whatever they're reflecting. This is why they are hard to identify as Reflectors. Even Reflectors don't recognise themselves as Reflectors when they first learn about Human Design. They often see themselves as the energy types of the people around them who they've been reflecting most of their lives.

Currently, there isn't a lot of detailed information about Reflectors and what it means to be one. Available information is often broad and lacks great examples that are relatable to many Reflectors. Reflectors need more guidance, advice, and lived examples about how to fully realise their potential and navigate their way through the many challenges within their design.

Reflectors from all over the world have called out too many times on social media platforms and within coaching sessions that they crave more tangible, specific information about how to navigate themselves through the world as a Reflector. Parents of Reflectors are craving solid advice about how to parent a healthy and happy Reflector who is usually very different from their other children. The Reflector voice, while faint at first, is finally being heard. Reflectors are calling out for a guide or a manual to help them understand how to live a more fulfilled and aligned life as a Reflector.

This book responds to this need. It provides Reflectors and those who love them with tangible actions Reflectors can take to work with their design so they can live a happy and healthy life.

A Reflector's journey is not an easy one nor a clear one. There is much they must traverse in order to realise their potential and step fully into their role. But their role is more essential than ever in these ever-changing times. Humanity needs their help.

Reflectors are here for others. They have an important role to play in the world as wise observers. Reflectors have great potential for wisdom through their nine, open energy centres. They need to show the world what is possible and what needs to change if people are to be awakened and follow a more enlightened path. Encouraging Reflectors to not only be themselves but to thrive as Reflectors, allows them to fully step into their purpose; to help move humanity forward.

Reflectors are being called right now to fulfil their design. When Reflectors understand themselves and how to work with their mechanics, they are fully tuned in to the world around them and they can safely ride the wave of life. They have the ability to read the tea leaves and sample and reflect what is going on around them. Reflectors can be strong and capable once they learn how to harness their rare design and work with it rather than against it.

With so much openness, and a different life trajectory to 99% of the population, Reflectors have some specific life challenges. If they learn to tackle these challenges and find ways to navigate their way through them, they can harness their strengths and fulfil their unique life purpose.

This book has five sections, each corresponding to an overarching strategy for Reflectors to deal with their challenges. While this isn't an exhaustive list, these sections are:

- Know Yourself
- Keep Healthy

- Connect with People
- Find Sustainable Work
- Deal with Pressure

This book is dedicated to helping you understand the challenges a Reflector faces and provides specific tips and techniques for managing each challenge so Reflectors can live as happy and healthy Reflectors.

My own personal experiences as a Reflector have been woven through the book to demonstrate real examples of these challenges and how they can be managed. I have learned to live as a happy, successful Reflector. I've experienced many of these things the hard way. This advice is shared with you because I've lived it personally and seen it work for others.

Reflectors need a lot of support to function as healthy human beings. They greatly benefit by having supportive, understanding people in their lives who help them live their potential and succeed in their role as Reflectors. Without this support, Reflectors have a hard time existing in this world.

While this book speaks specifically to Reflectors, anyone who knows or loves a Reflector can benefit from learning about these challenges and their possible solutions. We welcome you here and thank you for taking the time to read this book so you can get to know Reflectors better. Thank you for supporting Reflectors as they navigate their uniqueness. Reflectors can't do this without you. You are an important part of a Reflector's journey. Through you, Reflectors learn so much.

If you're a Reflector, it's time to step more fully into your role. To do this, you must first learn to deal with your challenges and work with your conditioning so you can become the best version of yourself and thrive as a Reflector.

This book offers you ways of navigating these challenges with the hope that they will help you as much as they have helped me.

Happy reading.

WHAT IS A HUMAN DESIGN REFLECTOR?

R EFLECTORS ARE DIFFERENT TO ALL other Human Design types. We have a unique decision-making strategy which requires us to take at least 28.5 days to make a big decision, truly ensuring that it feels right for us. This can be extremely difficult to do in a world that revolves around instant gratification. Waiting for something is a completely alien concept for most people; waiting a month can seem like a lifetime.

Not only do we have to wait a very long time to make a decision, we don't have the energy to get things done the way most other people do. Reflectors don't have access to sustainable life force and work force energy, unlike 70% of the population. Learning this can be quite deflating for Reflectors. For young Reflectors, these traits can seem daunting and life crippling. We can also be completely at the mercy of life conditioning.

Reflectors have all nine Human Design energy centres open in our chart. Each of our open centres absorbs the energy, thoughts, and emotions of the people and the world around us. This openness has the potential to make us very wise; we have the ability to see and feel who people really are. We can embody the health of the world around us and can sense how humanity is tracking. Through our sampling aura, we gain great wisdom and perspective about life.

With this complete openness, we also have the potential to become conditioned by the people and the world around us in every one of these energy centres and, therefore, in every part of ourselves. When we don't know how to release these absorbed energies, we hold onto them as though they are our own. Without knowing how to manage these energies, Reflectors can struggle in life.

WHAT IT MEANS TO BE COMPLETELY OPEN

E ACH OF THE NINE HUMAN DESIGN energy centres has a distinct role to play within us. When someone has an energy centre defined (coloured in), they have a consistent way of experiencing the energy and traits of that centre. When a centre is open, this energy is experienced inconsistently. Reflectors have all nine energy centres open and, therefore, experience a lot of inconsistent energy.

These open centres absorb and amplify energy from people who have this centre defined. Reflectors can amplify energy more intensely than the people they've absorbed energy from. Through our open centres, we experience all the different ways the energy of a defined centre can be expressed as we interact with people and the world around us.

When we don't understand the impacts of being completely open, we assume that the energy we experience in these centres is ours and we begin to identify with it. This is a major hurdle for Reflectors. It can be hard to distinguish between what is ours and what is being energetically absorbed from someone else.

Let's look at how each of the nine Human Design energy centres affect Reflectors by being open.

THE OPEN HEAD CENTRE

The Head centre is the gateway to the divine. This centre gives us a stream of ideas and inspiration. When the Head centre is open, we receive inspiration and ideas in many different ways. Our open Head centre allows us to engage with every possible way of thinking. Our imagination is without constraint. We can wonder and question the world without limitations. Ideas pop into our head at any given time. We even pick up ideas that don't belong to us- coming from the people around us.

The problem with having this centre open is that it becomes a pressure centre for us. The ideas keep flowing in, and we feel compelled to action and to understand them. We may also question where the ideas come from. We are often confused and suspicious about what pops into our heads which can make us doubt the validity of these ideas.

Like a bucket without a lid, thoughts and ideas bounce into our open Head centre causing us to constantly process them. We can lay awake at night with our minds on overdrive thinking, dreaming, and conceiving a myriad of ideas swirling around in our heads. It's hard to escape the pressure of the open Head centre. It can constantly keep us feeling wired and anxious, trying to solve and act on the contents of our heads.

THE OPEN AJNA CENTRE

The Ajna centre is a data processing centre. People who have a defined Ajna centre have a specific way of seeing the world. These people hold on to certainty about things and are often quite fixed in their views and beliefs. When two people with defined Ajna centres have opposing views, a conversation can quickly turn into a debate or an argument. Often, neither party is able to see things from the other person's perspective, and both are adamant that their view is correct.

Reflectors have this centre open which means we don't have a fixed way of thinking. We see things from multiple perspectives. We experience thinking from so many angles and perspectives that it's hard to be certain about anything. This can cause us to feel mentally lost at times. It can feel overwhelming and stressful not being certain about things because we can't hold onto a particular idea or belief.

We also absorb the thoughts and beliefs of the people around us. We often assume these thoughts and beliefs are our own. If we've grown up in an unhealthy environment with people who have destructive thoughts and beliefs, we begin to see the world through these limited and often negative perspectives. This can be detrimental to Reflectors.

Typically, it's only when Reflectors move away from influencing environments that we start to question our own beliefs and thoughts. Leaving home is a defining moment for a Reflector, when we're finally away from the conditioning thoughts and beliefs of the people we've spent most of our life with. These conditioned thoughts and beliefs begin to peel away. Slowly at first. Then, one day, we wonder how we ever thought these things at all.

For some Reflectors, these thoughts and beliefs are about simple things, like the way housework should be done or ideas about money or relationships. For other Reflectors, these thoughts and beliefs may have been fundamental to life: stout religious beliefs, cultural practices, or other fixed belief systems may have affected our entire existence up until that point. It's a life-altering moment when we realise that the thoughts we've spent our entire childhood believing are no longer correct for us. This can be both a liberating and a painful experience for Reflectors.

The Ajna centre makes Reflectors open-minded. We see the world through the limitless perspectives of the people within it. However, without an awareness about how our openness affects our thoughts, we can become greatly conditioned in the belief systems and thoughts of the people around us.

THE OPEN THROAT CENTRE

The Throat centre is the centre for communication and manifestation. People who have this centre defined communicate in a consistent way. They usually speak with a cadence that instils confidence and demands that other people listen.

With this centre open, a Reflector's power comes from listening and waiting. When we try to push with our voice, we struggle to be heard. We have two ears and one mouth for a reason. Through listening in silence, we learn more. We hear more and grow our wisdom through observation. When the timing is right and we're finally invited to speak, our voice and words have real impact. We can adjust our voice, tone, and words to communicate in a way that delivers a message which listeners hear as intended.

We live in a world where push communication is everywhere. We are encouraged to continually post on social media and push our voices out there so we can be heard and seen. We are told to speak up and speak out if we want to get noticed. But this doesn't work for Reflectors with our open Throat centre.

It takes great patience and effort not to talk when we have spent so much of our lives being encouraged to speak up. Working with the open Throat centre is one of the greatest challenges for a Reflector. When used properly, our open Throat centre can be one of the most powerful gifts we have. It can be used as a vessel for the wisdom we are here to share with the world.

THE OPEN G CENTRE

Our self-love, identity, and life-direction all come from the G centre. People with a defined G centre have a very distinct sense of self and a strong consistent identity. They are the same no matter where they are and who they are with. If you ask 50 people to describe a person with a defined G centre, their description will usually be very similar. They are who they are and that's that.

With this centre open, a Reflector's identity is adaptable and malleable. We change ourselves to become like the people we spend time with. We absorb the identity and direction of other people, which means we can associate and assimilate with many different personality types. If we're around someone who is a crazy adrenaline junkie, we may find ourselves jumping out of planes and climbing up mountains. When we're around people who are studious and intellectual, we may find ourselves sitting around talking about politics and books we've read. Sometimes we are perceived as being sweet and sensitive. Other times, we may seem wild and daring depending on how other people experience us.

I had a holiday romance when I was much younger with a man who said he couldn't pursue the romance past the holiday because I was too much of a party animal. Years later, when we bumped into each other again, he saw me in a much different environment and realised his perception of me was completely wrong. He'd met me during a crazy holiday time period. Despite telling him what I was like in my normal life, at the time, he couldn't see past my holiday identity.

We aren't faking it- we genuinely enjoy sampling and identifying with the people we're with at any one time. It's a beautiful thing to be able to fit in almost anywhere since we can adapt ourselves to most people and situations. It can, however, be difficult to define ourselves because we don't have a strong self-identity or clear life direction. We can strive for these things, but until we accept that this is not our design, life can be confusing and disappointing for Reflectors.

THE OPEN WILL CENTRE

The Will centre is about money, ego, and willpower. People with this centre defined have direct access to willpower. They also know their own value and are able to get things done even when the going gets tough.

Unfortunately, with this centre open, Reflectors don't have access to willpower in the traditional sense. Watching other people use their willpower to achieve things while we struggle can be extremely disappointing. We may have moments of willpower. In the presence of someone with a defined Will centre, we feel like we can achieve anything. However, once we're away from this person, borrowed willpower energy soon dissipates.

Our open Will centre also causes us to question our value. With so much inconsistency within us, it's easy to think that we don't add value anywhere. It can feel as though we have nothing to offer. This is disempowering for Reflectors. We can end up pushing with borrowed Will centre energy trying to prove ourselves and rationalise our value to others. This pushing can burn us out.

We must learn not to punish ourselves because we don't have access to consistent willpower energy. Learning to see our worth through our differences as Reflectors is key to valuing our openness for all the wisdom and knowledge it gives us. Our open Will centre allows us to sense what is truly valuable in life and this wisdom can guide us down the right life path.

THE OPEN SACRAL CENTRE

The Sacral centre provides life force and work force energy to 70% of the population who have it defined. These are Generator types. Generators have seemingly never-ending energy. They use this energy to literally build our world by working, raising families, and doing everything that is necessary for our evolution.

For the rest of us, including Reflectors, we don't have access to this consistent life force energy. We don't have energy to just keep going and going. At times, we can seem like the most energetic person in the room when we absorb this energy from others and amplify it. But, these bursts of energy aren't sustainable. If we continue to push ourselves with this borrowed energy, we will eventually burn ourselves out.

As younger Reflectors, we act as though we have all the energy in the world while we live off the energetic fumes of our Generator companions. We may even be able to live like this for the early part of our life. As we reach into our 30s and 40s, if we've continued to push with energy we don't have, we eventually get sick, depressed, or experience other ways of burnout that prevent us from accessing this borrowed life force energy.

For a Reflector to flourish in a world where we have limited access to life force energy, we must live differently than most other people. We must learn to pay attention to our inner need to take things slow, get plenty of rest, and stop pushing with borrowed energy so we can sustain ourselves and fulfil our purpose. When we do this, we tap into the wisdom our open Sacral centre gives us about workload, 'doing' energy, and sexuality.

THE OPEN SPLEEN CENTRE

The Spleen centre is where our instinct for survival lives. It's about survival in the now and it impacts time, health, and intuition. Those that have this centre defined have access to feel-good energy. They have an inner sense of time and a fixed, powerful immune system. They also have consistent access to intuitive insights in the moment.

With the Spleen centre open, it affects Reflectors in many ways. It gives us a very sensitive immune system. This is an early warning signal that tells us when something isn't right within us. It signals that we need to pay attention to our health before something more serious or life threatening happens. The Spleen centre being open causes us to experience more health issues, such as allergies and intolerances, than people who have this centre defined.

Reflectors don't have access to the feel-good energy that this centre provides. We are, therefore, attracted to people with a defined Spleen centre because we feel good around them. We may become co-dependent and have a hard time letting these people go, trying to hold on to this feel good energy. We can also become attached to things that make us feel good and have a hard time letting these things go as well.

Our open Spleen centre gives us a very fluid relationship with time. We easily loose connection with time by being so in the flow. We may also struggle with grasping our intuitive abilities because we don't experience intuition in a consistent way. This can cause us to doubt whether we are intuitive at all, if we don't truly tap into the many different ways we experience intuition.

Every gate within the Spleen centre can be expressed as fear. This fear helps us ensure our survival. We easily become overwhelmed by fear when we have this centre open. We also pick up on the fears and anxiety of people around us. Without being able to differentiate between what we are experiencing ourselves and what is being absorbed from other people, we can become deeply impacted by the fears of the Spleen.

On a positive note, we are super tuned in to other people because of our openness here. We can sense fear and anxiety in others and may even know when someone else is ill. This centre allows us to become wise by giving us the ability to be sensitive and tuned in to the health and survival of both ourselves and the people around us.

THE OPEN SOLAR PLEXUS CENTRE

The Solar Plexus is the centre for emotional energy. People who have this centre defined have an emotional wave. These waves are emotional highs and lows which allow these people to become clear about what is right for them across their wave. People who have this centre defined can use their wave to determine what they want to create in life.

With this centre open, Reflectors don't have access to this emotional wave which provides clarity about what is right for us. Instead, our openness makes us highly empathetic as well as vulnerable to the emotions of other people. Reflectors absorb other people's emotions and then amplify this emotional energy back out. Sometimes, this causes us to seem like an extremely emotional person.

Our openness in this centre makes us want to please everyone so that we don't upset them. We don't want to stir up other people's emotional energy because this ultimately impacts us. We feel their emotional energy. When we keep people happy, we can control the affect their emotional energy has on us. Of course, keeping everyone happy isn't always the best way forward.

Our ability to be empathetic enables us to feel someone's emotional state often before they notice it or express it. We can use this ability to tune into others, to connect with them, and work with their emotional energy.

THE OPEN ROOT CENTRE

The Root centre is about adrenaline energy and divine timing. For people who have this centre defined, things get done when they get done. These people have a consistent way of experiencing adrenaline energy and they're usually immune to stress. They have an energetic adrenaline pulse which is either on or off. When the pulse is on, they have the energy to do something. When the pulse is off, the adrenaline energy stops and so do they. When they follow this pulse to do or not do, they set themselves up for success.

For Reflectors, having this centre open means we don't have an on and off pulse. Instead, we have a continuous stream of pressure to do with no clear internal off button. This causes us to always feel under pressure to get things done so we can be free of the pressure and stress to 'do.' Unfortunately, we create for ourselves a never-ending to-do list.

We also pick up pressure from people who have a defined Root centre even if they aren't actually pressuring us to do something. We feel and sense their pressure centre energy, and it pushes us further to get things done.

When we harness this energy, we learn what stressors are our own and which ones have been placed on us externally. Learning to understand the cause of this pressure and finding techniques to reduce stress are essential for Reflectors to enable good health and sustainability. Our openness here helps us determine what pressure-based activities are worthy of undertaking and which should be left off our to-do list so we can live a more stress-free life.

With so much openness, Reflectors have a lot of challenges to contend with.

AN ANALOGY OF OPENNESS

L ET'S CONSIDER EACH HUMAN DESIGN energy
centre a box. The open centres are empty boxes without
a lid. The defined centres are boxes overflowing with fruit.
Even though two people may have the same defined centre,
they have different fruit in their box. One person's box may
be overflowing with oranges and another person's box may be
overflowing with apples.

Using this analogy, Reflectors are walking around with
nine empty open boxes. When we spend time with other
people, some of the fruit from their overflowing boxes spill
into our open boxes. This seems pleasant enough. It gives us
the ability to taste and sample the different types of fruit from
other people's boxes.

This becomes troubling when we cling onto the fruit
instead of letting it bounce back out of our box. Our boxes
aren't designed to hold fruit for long so if we don't learn to
enjoy the fruit for a moment and then let it go, we can end up
with a full box of mixed rotting fruit.

Having completely open boxes can feel like there's nothing juicy and tasty within us. We can feel empty at times. This emptiness can cause us to wonder just who we are and why we are here. We can sometimes crave the fruit from other people's defined boxes.

We need to realise that we aren't actually just a bunch of empty boxes. Instead, we are a fruit salad bowl. We can sample each different fruit that pops in and out of our empty boxes. When we do this, we begin to explore the magic and awesomeness that comes with being a Reflector. Not only are we here to taste the many different types of fruit, we're here to gain an understanding of how the individual fruit contributes to the enjoyment of the whole fruit salad and to share our taste experiences with everyone else who can only experience the fruit they have access to within their defined boxes.

The trick for Reflectors is to take a bite of each fruit and then let it bounce out of the box, so we don't end up with a permanent box of sour fruit.

PART ONE

Know Yourself

TO BE EFFECTIVE AND FULFIL our unique role as Reflectors, we first need to understand our own mechanics. We need to understand what makes us different from other people, how to navigate our uniqueness, and how to recognise our strengths so we can confidently step into our Reflector shoes.

The biggest challenge we have as a Reflector is to accept ourselves for being very different from everyone else. We often try extremely hard to fit in and be like other people. But we simply aren't designed like most other people. By acknowledging our differences and not punishing ourselves for being this way, we can get closer to self-acceptance and allow ourselves to grow into our unique design.

We have a few specific challenges that we need to work with on our path to self-discovery and acceptance.

This section has seven main challenges:

- People pleasing
- Life conditioning
- Identity crisis
- Becoming a human barometer
- Living with fear
- Lack of energy
- Linear time

Each chapter within this section is dedicated to exploring one of these challenges and provides tips for effectively connecting with yourself.

THE CHALLENGE OF PEOPLE PLEASING

*People who are the most difficult to please
are often the least worth pleasing.*

- unknown

REFLECTORS FEEL WHEN SOMEONE is happy, angry, or upset through the open emotional Solar Plexus centre. We feel other people's emotional energy and adjust our behaviour accordingly. Reflectors strive to make everyone else happy. When others feel happy, we feel happy. For this reason, we say and do whatever we can to please other people and ensure we don't stir up their low emotional energy.

Reflectors regularly become people pleasers and conflict avoiders as a strategy to keep the peace. We put the needs of other people ahead of our own needs and this can cause problems for not only ourselves but within our relationships.

Being in touch with other people's feelings and wanting to make them happy is a wonderful gift. However, this becomes a problem when we continually suppress our own needs as a Reflector for the benefit of others.

Trying to be nice to everyone all the time and ensuring people stay in a positive emotional state can be exhausting. Not only is this exhausting, but we can feel like we are forever treading on eggshells around other people and not being ourselves.

I've been in relationships where I've completely given up things that I love in order to make the other person happy. I've sacrificed where I've lived and my work to try and please my partner and help them sustain a happy emotional state.

Reflectors often enable other people to 'get their way' in order to minimize conflict and to protect the emotional state of the other person. This can become normalised in Reflectors' relationships. We can hold off voicing our own needs and become agreeable to all the wants and needs of our partners.

Making small sacrifices to avoid conflict has its benefits in some circumstances.

When my husband and I go to the cinema, we usually end up watching an action movie because I feel how happy that makes him. I also find it hard to sit next to someone at the cinema sensing that they'd prefer to be watching something else. It's not an enjoyable experience for me. When my husband is enjoying the movie, even if I'm not loving it, it's a more enjoyable experience. This is because I can deal with my own lack of enjoyment better than I can deal with my husband's bored and frustrated energy.

If we are always agreeable with our partners about where to go for dinner, where to spend our holidays, what animal to buy as a pet, and so on, the other person will start believing that we enjoy the same things they enjoy and gain a false sense of who we are. It may come as a shock when they finally learn that we are not who they think we are and, ultimately, both parties become resentful.

While conflict avoidance is advantageous, a certain amount of conflict is healthy and necessary in life. Conflict allows both parties to air their truth and verbalize their needs. Conflict teaches people to be flexible and to listen. Ultimately, conflict leads to solutions through communication and a resolution that allows us to compromise around our differences.

When we give in to the needs of another person because we don't want to upset them, we teach them two things.

1. That their needs are more important than our needs.
2. That we want and like the same things they do.

Small sacrifices are beneficial. When we sacrifice our own needs entirely for years, however, it can eventually all become too much. In a single moment, we can undo a relationship by revealing how we feel about everything we have thus far been agreeable to.

Our agreeableness enables them to see us in a way that isn't really us. When this all comes undone, they realise they have no idea about what we really like and who we really are. This can not only strain the relationship; it can break it.

Conflict avoidance and people pleasing can also deny us the important benefits of engaging in conflict with others so we can learn more about each other and find a relationship that is mutually beneficial.

SOLUTION – PROTECT YOURSELF

———— ▱ ————

W E WILL ALWAYS PICK UP on the emotional energy of other people regardless of how much we try not to. We can't change this. What we can do is use our emotional sensors as a guidance system. We can tune in to other people's emotions and do what we can to navigate a situation as long as we aren't sacrificing our own needs in the process.

We can't keep everyone happy all of the time. Having some conflict can be a healthy way of negotiating the boundaries of a relationship. The most important tactic we can employ as a Reflector is to learn to be a screen and not a sponge when we sample other people's emotions.

This means instead of soaking up other people's emotional energy, you should feel the emotion and then let it pass right through you like it's passing through a screen with tiny holes in it. Sample other people's emotions so you're aware of them but don't hold onto them and let these emotions become you. This means that you shouldn't make decisions and choices based solely on other people's emotional needs. This doesn't lead to a healthy relationship. Let the emotion's you sample from other people guide and shape your response. Don't let them change your response.

At times, you should use this guidance to keep the peace and avoid conflict. However, this should not be something you do on every occasion because you want to please everyone else and always keep them happy.

It's time to start acknowledging your own needs. Just because you feel other people's emotions and can adapt yourself accordingly, doesn't mean you should. Allow yourself to express your needs in spite of the emotional energy you feel from other people and don't be afraid to speak your truth.

I still choose movies to watch at the cinema that my husband wants to watch. However, when we're home and he wants to watch sports or something I don't feel like watching, I now rarely sit there and watch it with him. Instead, I choose to do something else that I enjoy doing rather than sit there in silence because it makes him feel happy.

There's nothing wrong with having different desires and pleasures and expressing them. It contributes to the development of a healthy relationship. When we feel free to express what we want, despite how it makes the other person feel, it is liberating. This also helps us find our independence and form relationships with people who accept us for our differences, rather than with people who like us because we're always agreeable and catering to their needs.

When we let our empathetic ability steer our ship, we will always head in a direction that suits the passengers we pick up rather than taking our natural course and going with the flow of the wind. Trying to please everyone all the time eventually burns us out. Having empathy and feeling the emotional energy of other people is a wonderful gift that we can use to tune in to the world around us. We just need to protect ourselves from the turbulence of the emotional wind along the way to ensure that we don't sink our own ship.

COACHING TIPS

1. BE A SCREEN NOT A SPONGE

Sponges absorb fluids. They soak them up and hold onto them. This is great for the purpose of being a sponge. Like a sponge, Reflectors absorb energy from people nearby, 'soaking it up' in the same way. While this soaking up action is helpful to a sponge's purpose, it is not healthy for Reflectors. When you soak up energy, you can quickly become afflicted by the energy and assume it as your own. This can ultimately lead you to burn out.

Instead, Reflectors should act like a screen, allowing the emotional energy of other people to flow through you so you feel and sample this energy but then let it pass right through and out of you. This way, you don't hold onto these emotions, mistake them for your own, and then amplify them back out more intensely.

When you act like a screen rather than a sponge, you allow yourself to become wise about emotional energy. We prevent yourself from becoming caught up in emotions that don't belong to us. We no longer lose your own needs in the process of making everyone else happy.

2. SPEAK YOUR TRUTH

When you learn to be a screen rather than a sponge, you not only protect yourself from being caught up in other people's emotional energy, you also give yourself permission to be you. When you're no longer overwhelmed and at the effect of other people's low emotional energy, you can finally make choices that include meeting your own needs.

Armed with this wisdom, when faced with conflict and the possibility of affecting other people's emotions, you should speak your truth, vocalise your needs, and not be at the mercy of other people's emotional energy. Like a screen, you should let it pass right through and out of you again.

Conflict avoidance and people pleasing has its time and place. When you're effectively screening other people's emotions, you will sense when these times are warranted. At all other times, ensure you look after your own needs and speak your own truth.

THE CHALLENGE OF
LIFE CONDITIONING

Authenticity is a collection of choices that we have to make every day. It's about the choice to show up and be real. The choice to be honest. The choice to let our true selves be seen.
- Brené Brown

REFLECTORS ARE SHAPED by the people we spend the most time with. This includes our families, friends, colleagues, and whoever we live with. Through our open centres, we absorb other people's energy, thoughts, feelings, and perceptions. During our childhood, these people can deeply condition who we become.

Growing up can be a very confusing time for a Reflector. We may struggle to find our own identity because we constantly absorb so much from everyone else. Without knowing that these energetic experiences don't actually belong to us, we begin to identify with them as if they are our own. This is what conditioning means; we become conditioned to believe that we own the thoughts, feelings, and energies absorbed from the people around us.

By the time we reach adulthood, we may still have no clear idea of who we really are. Being such sensitive, open beings, it is difficult to tell which parts of ourselves are authentically ours and which thoughts, feelings, and beliefs are just reflections of the people and the world around us.

Our amplification of other people's energies can also cause people to have strong, mistaken ideas about who we are. When Reflectors are around Generator types, for example, we can take in the Generator's sacral energy. We then amplify this energy back out, seeming as though we have a lot of energy ourselves. We can outperform them energetically when this happens. Understandably, people may mistakenly think we have a lot more energy than we actually do. When people don't understand our sampling and amplifying nature, they see us as whatever we amplify – in this example, they see us as highly energetic.

I've been the first person to reach the top of a mountain when climbing with Generator friends. Their sacral energy gives me a huge boost to get to the top first. It seems like I'm the fittest of them, given my ability to reach the top before them. But, this is really not the case. If I was alone, I would just meander up the mountain or possibly not even have the motivation to climb it at all. Their perceptions are formed by the way they see me act when around them.

It is impossible for people to know that, as Reflectors, we are similar to chameleons, changing with the people around us. While this is an unconscious reflex for Reflectors, it can be hard for other people to grasp.

Our parents and caregivers are highly influential to how we perceive ourselves as Reflectors. They contribute to both the positive and negative perceptions we have of ourselves simply by being in our presence. If we grew up with an angry and emotional father, we most likely absorbed these emotions and amplified them during our childhood. We probably made an assumption that this anger we felt as a child was our own and thus began to identity with it. Similarly, if we grew up living with a mother who was constantly demonstrating a complete lack of self-worth, we likely adopted a lack of self-worth for ourselves. Reflectors are greatly impacted by the way we are bought up and the people who surround us.

During my childhood, my mother was doting and extremely caring, but she had a strong will due to her defined Will centre. When we argued, we fought tooth and nail. She refused to back down, so I became even more strong-willed in these situations. Eventually, mum would give up trying to argue with me because I dug my heels in against her defined will.

Not only do we reflect back the energy of our family, but we also amplify it. This means we often reflect back a more intense version of this energy, thought, or feeling than the person we absorbed it from. For example, if our mother is religious, we may amplify her beliefs and appear even more devout then she is. When we're in an argument with another person who is expressing anger, we will often amplify this anger back at them even more dramatically than the person expressing it. For this reason, we can be seen to be more 'emotional' or 'dramatic' through the eyes of others.

Amplifying the energies of parents and siblings can strongly shape how we think of ourselves and what we believe in. This amplification of energy can also shape how people around us perceive us. When we amplify the negative emotions picked up from our parents, they may see us as the problem child rather than realizing the we are merely a reflection of their relationship. It becomes hard to disentangle ourselves from these perceptions when our parents also perceive us through these amplifications. They can further fuel this misconception by labelling us with terms like 'problem child.'

Without awareness, we're often ignorant to the way we amplify the energy, thoughts, and feelings of people while we are living with them. We may not realise that we've become conditioned to think and feel a particular way until we are no longer living with the person who has energetically conditioned us. Using the above example, we might have to leave the family home and live alone for a while to realise that we aren't really religious at all and our devoutness is purely an amplification of our mother's religious beliefs.

When Reflectors finally discover this sampling nature and how so much of who we are has been conditioned by other people, it can feel completely liberating as well as overwhelmingly distressful. Navigating ourselves through this period of awakening can feel scary while we begin to disentangle ourselves from the years of misconceptions about the feelings, thoughts, and energies we believed were our own.

It can take time to unravel ourselves from our conditioning to reveal our true nature. But, we must do this if we are to blossom as Reflectors and become the person we were born to be.

SOLUTION – DISCHARGE YOUR CONDITIONING

We are not our conditioning. Nor are we designed to live as conditioned beings. We have a natural Teflon aura that can protect us from these conditioning forces once we understand how to use it properly. We cannot avoid the conditioning of the greater world around us and the impact of the planetary transits, but we can learn to protect ourselves from other people's conditioning influences using this resistant Teflon aura.

Before we can truly tap into our ability to resist the conditioning energies of the people around us, we must first learn to recognise and release any current conditioning. Reflectors need to take time away from other people to establish the difference between our nature and our conditioning. We need to break free of these conditioning patterns and unveil our true selves.

If we've been living with someone for a very long time, we need to remove ourselves from them for long enough to notice how we feel when they're not around. This can take time. Spending a couple of nights away won't give us enough time to completely disconnect from their energy and to notice the conditioning we may have picked up from them over time.

The longer we've lived with someone, the longer time we may need away from them to separate ourselves from their conditioning. Ideally, taking a few weeks or a month apart can help us to really separate from their energy and to properly notice how we feel and think when they're not around. Taking this opportunity to learn about ourselves is totally worth the effort required to take the time away.

When we do choose to take time away from the influence of others, it's important that we don't substitute one person's conditioning for another's. For example, leaving one partner to move straight in with another typically won't give us the space we need away from other people's energy to clearly identify what is us and what is not us. We need to give ourselves as much time as necessary to find ourselves and be free of our conditioning.

In my 20s, I had a series of two-year relationships with exactly a year off between each. Each of these relationships were unhealthy and were with men who had been damaged in one way or another. When I was single again, living alone, I always seemed to be healthier and happier, but I didn't understand why. I thought finding a partner and having a relationship was the main focus in life, so I kept on my pursuit to find someone else instead of going on a journey in search of myself.

It took me about a year on my own to begin to recover from these relationships and to start to find myself again. Just as I started to make some healthy progress on separating myself from the partner in the previous relationship, I'd meet someone else and fall straight into a live-in relationship again. I never gave myself enough time or a proper chance to recover from these relationships. I didn't allow myself to truly unravel from the toxicity of those bonds.

If you choose to take time away from someone to explore yourself properly and you must live with someone during this period, make sure you at least have your own bedroom and plenty of alone time. The more time we have on our own, the more we can connect with our true selves. This gives us a proper gauge about the energy we have picked up from other people.

Once you learn how to tell the difference between your energy and energy that's been picked up from other people, remember to be a screen not a sponge. Let the energy from other people pass through you so you feel it, but don't let it stay within you so that it defines you. This is what is meant by having a Teflon aura: energy can touch you, but it doesn't have to stick to you.

The more practice you have discharging and releasing energy you've picked up from other people, the easier and quicker it gets. With practice, you can learn to discharge this energy in minutes. The key is to separate yourself physically from the source of the energy so you can properly release it.

One of the best ways to discharge energy is to spend time out in nature. When we're in nature we feel more connected to ourselves. We draw from the revitalizing and unconditional energy of nature to help clear our minds, bodies, and auras of the energetic junk we've picked up from other people in our daily lives.

Travel is an effective and therapeutic way to explore the natural world. Travel not only discharges other people's energy, it helps us to revitalise our own energetic resources.

I love escaping on my own to places of natural beauty. Beaches, rainforests, and mountains all give me the opportunity to reflect and have the space to notice myself without the influence of other people energetically.

This doesn't necessarily mean we have to travel completely alone. Travelling with other people can also work as long as you sleep alone to gain the full therapeutic effect of travel. If you choose to travel somewhere with another person for this purpose, make sure you have your own bedroom, or better yet, have your own hotel room. This will give you time and space at the end of each day to discharge their energy and be with yourself. Travelling with a partner, family, or a friend and staying together in the same room doesn't give you the space you need to bask in your own aura and fully discharge the energy of others.

Every time I need to do some soul searching in my life, I travel somewhere new and naturally beautiful. My life has been dotted with travel adventures that helped me make needed transitions in my life. I travelled at the end of all my relationships. Yes...I had a few bad ones. I travelled the day after I finished high school and left my childhood home. I travelled when I finished university. This is how I ended up on safari in Africa, chasing waterfalls in Northern Australia, sailing around the Greek Islands, and many other adventures. I still travel when I feel stuck about what to do next in my life. These breaks in time when I spend a few weeks connecting with the natural world help me reconnect with myself and find calmness and beauty within.

Reflectors need a balance between being alone and having people around. Too much time alone isn't necessarily a good thing because we need people and the world around us to energetically activate us. We're not designed to be complete hermits. If we lock ourselves away from other people for too long, it can become difficult to get back out there again. The thought of mixing with other people can feel overwhelming. This is one of the reasons why it isn't healthy for Reflectors to spend too much time alone.

For this reason, I've found that one of the best ways to travel as a Reflector is with small group adventure tour companies. This type of travel is typically more nature-focused than traditional group tours and they're usually not so adventurous that you need to be a mountaineer to join them.

Adventure tour companies offer small group tours in most places around the world. I always join these as a solo traveller with my own room. On these tours, I have the companionship of a tour leader and a few fellow travellers who start out as strangers and usually end up as friends.

These tours are a perfect platform for my self-discovery. I don't waste too much energy working out where to go and what to do on these trips because most activities are preplanned and the tour leader offers great ideas for any spare time I may have. Having my own room gives me plenty of time alone when I need it. There is also time to connect with people as often as I like. And, there is always someone to go to dinner with when I don't feel like eating alone.

The wonderful thing about travelling like this is that I meet like-minded people, who are generally energetically positive and seeking their own soulful experience. This is wonderful energy for a Reflector to be around and absorb. I've spent many moments staring at beautiful sunsets in silence with an almost stranger. While I'm having my own unique experience, I also recognise the energetic connection between the two of us without any emotional baggage. I highly recommend travelling this way if the thought of travelling completely alone doesn't appeal to you.

When I travel with a partner or even friends, my travel experiences are seldomly as therapeutic. My experience is often tainted by the person I am with. If they aren't having a good time, if we've had a disagreement, or if perhaps they just don't want to do what I want to do, these getaways are nowhere near as beneficial. Most of the time, when I travel with someone else, I feel disappointed. They don't necessarily receive as many benefits from these travel experiences as I do. I am disappointed because I feel constrained by them. I feel constrained by them because I usually can't just do and see what I feel like doing. I am constrained by their emotional energy and their personal energetic experience. I am constrained because I'm not as free to just be in my own flow as I am alone on these expeditions, and my own experience is marred by them.

Travelling alone like this may sound lonely, but I can promise you it's not. Instead, you meet a rich tapestry of new people and places that you can sample energetically. It's an extraordinarily enriching experience for a Reflector.

Self-discovery journeys help Reflectors to unveil who we truly are, what we like, what inspires us, and where our interests lie. It's an awakening and magnificent process. Once we find ourselves, we begin to understand what conditioning we need to let go of so we can find our own bliss. This process helps us discover the things that make us happiest. Once we find ourselves underneath all of that conditioning, we can establish the people and places that feel best for us and find clarity about the things we truly enjoy doing. We can then fully utilise our Teflon aura, no longer at the mercy of other people's conditioning influences.

Coaching Tips

1. SPEND TIME ALONE

Whenever you can, find time alone so you can discharge the energy you've absorbed from other people. Find a space that feels good which helps you disconnect from other people and just be with yourself.

Getting into nature is a powerful way that helps us discharge this energy. Spending time out in mother nature is wonderful therapy for Reflectors because we energetically connect into the living ecosystem and we can more easily release energies that don't belong to us.

Nature activities that help with discharging energy include:

- Walking or sitting on the beach
- Sitting in a garden with your bare feet touching the earth
- Swimming in the ocean
- Hiking on a nature trail
- Riding a bike through the countryside
- Paddling a canoe on a lake
- Sitting on a cabin patio in the middle of the forest

The list of activities you can do to spend time in nature is endless. Whatever you choose, ensure it's something that you enjoy doing.

2. GET AWAY TO KNOW YOURSELF

When you can, regularly spend time away from the people you normally live with. The longer you can get away, the greater chance you'll have of discharging all of their energy. A few days is helpful, a few weeks is better. While you're away, you'll be able to reconnect with yourself away from their conditioning influence and be able to release their energy completely.

Get away on your own

If you can get away on your own, do it. Time completely alone can be wonderful medicine for Reflectors. If you go away for this purpose, make sure you are completely away from the influence of other people's energy and any life stressors.

Going on a working holiday alone may not be the best way to discharge your energy if you are under work stress. The purpose of your time alone is to just BE. You shouldn't be doing too much. If you are going to do something during this time away, make sure the activity isn't too energetically distracting.

For example. if you're an experienced horse rider, going on a horse-riding adventure may be wonderful therapy for your time alone, allowing you to really be in the moment.If you've never ridden a horse before, this type of activity will likely be stressful and consuming. You'll be so focused on operating the horse, ensuring your own safety, you'll have little time for self-reflection allowing yourself to just BE in the moment.

Get away with other people

If you can't get away on your own or this doesn't sound appealing, go away somewhere with other people. It's best if these people aren't the people you normally live with and they are people who you generally feel good around. Remember, you will sample the energy of whoever you're around, so if you travel with people who don't feel good you will absorb these lower energies.

Every time I travel with someone else, my experience is impacted by them. If I want to sit and watch the sunset with them and they're feeling impatient or not overly interested, my own sunset experience is affected by their energetic presence. Now, when I travel with friends and family, I use this as holiday time with them only. This doesn't count as therapeutic time away to discharge energy and restore myself.

A fabulous alternative for getaways with other people that can still be therapeutic is small group adventure tours. Book a tour as a single person and make sure you have your own room. This type of getaway allows you to remove yourself completely from everyone who normally impacts you energetically, so you can discharge their energy and be with yourself. When you feel like it, you can still connect with other people who won't impact you as much energetically as familiar friends and family.

3. NOTICE WHAT IS YOU AND WHAT IS NOT YOU

During your time alone, begin to notice where your thoughts go, what you sense, and how you feel. The longer you spend alone, the more you will notice. While you're experiencing life in the now, without the influence of other people, you may begin to notice thoughts, feelings, and emotions that you've absorbed from other people just peel away. Your thoughts may drift in a different direction than usual. You may start to see things from a different perspective. The more you do this, the more you peel away. Eventually, you should be able to peel away the layers of conditioning right down to those you absorbed during childhood.

As you begin to unravel from your conditioning, your true self begins to emerge. This is why it's so important to just be in the moment during these times. You may decide to take a walk, visit a museum, build a campfire, or whatever else compels you while in your own space. If you can, allow yourself to go with the flow.

Find a way to process this. You may choose to write in a journal or record yourself speaking about it. You may just make mental notes that you can draw upon later. This should be a cathartic process. It should help you notice what belongs to you and what is just your conditioning so you can finally release it.

4. MAKE BETTER CHOICES

When you return from your getaway and you're back among people, you should start to notice how you change when in other people's presence and when you're picking up their energies, thoughts, and feelings. You can then practice being a screen, using your Teflon aura. Notice these energies as you sample them but let them fall off you, so they don't become you.

Armed with this ability and knowledge about what is you and what is not you, you also have the opportunity to make better life choices. You can begin to release conditioning influences that are no longer serving you and let go of the thoughts, feelings, and energies that were never really your own.

This can be a huge awakening process, especially if you realise you've been living someone else's life. For example, you may realise that you are passionate about helping people but not really passionate about science in the way you thought you were. This may cause you to reconsider whether that science degree you're doing at university is actually right for you. Your father may have been an avid science fan who wished he'd studied science when he was younger. You may realise that choosing this degree was caused by his unconscious conditioning. You now have the opportunity to change your degree and life direction. Perhaps you'll choose a degree that involves helping people if this is what you discover you're passionate about.

If you realise that the person you live with is actually quite toxic for you and you feel so compromised around them that you can't be your true wonderful self, then this may be the time you decide to part ways or at least move out.

Working out what is yours and what is not yours can help you make changes in your life that allow you to be the purest, unconditioned, most authentic expression of yourself.

THE CHALLENGE OF IDENTITY CRISIS

Think back to a place that you loved…feels good doesn't it?
                                                    - Unknown

OUR LIFE DIRECTION COMES from our G centre located in the middle of the Human Design body chart. The G centre is also where we find our identity and our sense of self. Reflectors have the G centre open, so it absorbs and amplifies the identity and direction of other people. This means our life direction is changeable and we don't have a strong and consistent sense of self. This gives us the ability to become social chameleons, adapting to and identifying with the people around us. We wear many different hats across our lifetime. We have a fluid identity and easily go with the flow in the moment. We typically have many different types of friends for this reason who we mirror and naturally adapt ourselves to accordingly.

My husband has a defined G centre. This means he has a clear identity and life direction. When I first met his friends and family, they all defined him in the same way. No matter whether they played with him on the school ground as children or worked with him later in life, his traits and life path were described consistently by everyone. He is who he is and that is that. His identity and direction are undeniably clear and consistent. He's been the same way his whole life.

When my husband met my friends, he noticed that they're all undeniably different. They come from many different walks of life. Their impressions and descriptions of me are different. Their perspectives about who I am have been shaped by the circumstances of our relationship and the period of life we spent together. Some describe me as wild and loud, while others see me as more soulful and chilled out. None of them know exactly what work I am doing at any moment or what I will do next. Even my father, in his wedding speech, said that he thought my life would head a particular way and, so far, it has gone in a surprisingly different direction.

When we don't understand this energy, we often feel lost. Other people seem to have a clear sense of who they are and where they're going while we struggle to find clarity within ourselves. This causes us to question if we're loveable. Even when we do find an identity or direction that feels right at the time, this doesn't stick around for long. We change as often as the wind and holding onto one particular identity or direction is something that just isn't in our design.

Without awareness, our identity and direction can become intertwined with the people we spend the most time with, and it becomes difficult to tell the difference between them and us. We often struggle to find our authentic self. We can also wind up living someone else's life, following their dreams and their passions, and assuming their identity. If we assume the identity and direction of someone who is a positivity magnet, this can feel great. If this person has low self-worth, it can have a devasting effect on how we perceive ourselves.

We often struggle to separate ourselves from the people we live with and the people with whom we spend the greatest amount of time. Therefore, our environment and the people within it have a huge impact on who we are and how we see ourselves.

Solution – Find Your Right Place and Right People

It is crucial for a Reflectors' health and wellbeing to spend time with the right people in the right places. Because we absorb the G centre energy of other people, we need to be around people who have a positive and loving sense of self and life direction. We need people in our lives who bring out the best in us. Their healthy sense of self has a positive influence on us as we absorb this energy and amplify it back out.

There are some people in our lives who we must spend time with, such as family and work colleagues. While we can't remove some people completely from our lives when they aren't good for us, we can reduce the amount of time we spend with them or at least develop strategies to cope more effectively when in their presence.

Our environment is also vitally important. We need to be in places that help us feel good. Being in the right place with the right people allows us to thrive in life, in our relationships, and within our careers.

The 'right place' is a physical location that simply feels good for us. This is a place we enjoy being where we feel happy and content. The right place is not just where we live but also where we spend any amount of time. Being in the wrong place will bother someone with an open G centre much more than someone with a defined G centre.

When I dine out with my husband, I sometimes end up in a seat that doesn't feel right. In the past, I wouldn't say anything. I'd sit there feeling uncomfortable and bothered for the duration of the meal. I never said anything because I didn't want to upset anyone. Typically, my silence caused me to have an unpleasant dining experience. Feeling uncomfortable and not quite right, I'd often end up in a disagreement with my husband, the food would be problematic, or things would just feel 'off.'

I no longer sit in silence when I don't feel comfortable. Today, I voice how I feel. To my relief, it turns out my husband doesn't really care where he sits. I now choose my seat in restaurants and tell him when I don't feel right. He's realised that when I feel good, dining is an overall better experience for both of us. Now, he insists that I choose where I sit which enables both of us to have a better time.

Sitting in the wrong place for lunch is something most Reflectors can put up with. It might not be a pleasant experience, but we can live with it if we have to. What is far tougher to live with is being in a home, workplace, or other location where we spend a regular amount of time that doesn't feel good to us.

FEEL GOOD AT HOME

When our home doesn't feel good, we may experience dis-ease while at home. Our relationships suffer, or we feel unproductive and unmotivated to do anything. A place that doesn't feel good isn't our 'right place.'

If you love basking in sunlight, but you live in a basement with very little natural light, this is probably not your 'right place.' If you adore the cold and snow, but you live in the tropics, this is likely not your right place. If you love colour and texture, but you live in a stark, completely white apartment, this may not be your right place.

You will innately feel good when a place is right for you. When you love where you live, you look forward to sitting on your balcony or snuggling up in a blanket on your couch. There will be occasions you don't feel like being there, but generally, it should feel good to spend time in your home.

Does the thought of home make you happy? If home makes you feel stressed, sad, or some other negative emotion, it is unlikely that this is your right place. It is very hard to pull yourself into a higher vibration when you don't feel good where you are.

If you've realized that your home is not your right place and you have the opportunity to move somewhere else, do it! Living in your right place is one of the most empowering things a Reflector can do to enable an enjoyable and healthy life experience.

If moving is not an option, do your best to make a space within your home that feels right for you. This could be your bedroom, your office, or even your garden that you can groom in a way that makes you feel happy when you spend time there. You can even try moving the furniture around and use Feng Shui techniques to alter the way your home is furnished.

My home office never quite felt right. I spent a lot of time there, but I always felt stifled. One day, I knocked a hole in the wall of my office and put in a window. This allowed me to look out from my desk at the garden, and it let in much more light. My office is now my sanctuary and I love spending time there.

Ultimately, finding a home that feel's right for you is one of the most effective things a Reflector can do to live a happy and healthy life. Whatever it takes, this should be a priority. All

Reflectors need a sanctuary where you can go to rest, unwind, discharge the energy of others, and just bask in feeling good.

FEEL GOOD AT WORK

When we work in a location that doesn't feel right, this can also negatively impact our life. We spend so much time at work, it's vital that it feels good. If your workplace doesn't feel good, do what you can to change it. If it feels really bad, it may be time to look for another job. If this isn't an option, change what you can. Try to change where your desk is located, who you're sitting next to, or ask to move to a totally different office location.

At the very least, you can put objects and images in your work area that make you feel happy, or perhaps you can change things around so that the workspace feels better. It is imperative that you do what you can to make this space feel right for you. Especially if you spend more than a few hours there each day.

When I write, it is extremely important that I write in a place of visual beauty. While I love my home office, it's not my right place for creative writing. I've tried many times to write at home, but I ultimately get writer's block or my words stop making sense. I also spend more time attending to distractions than I do typing words on a page.

For my writing to flow, I need to be somewhere that has a view and lots of fresh air. This is usually from an apartment balcony near the beach. This right place allows words to stream out when I'm writing. Sometimes, my fingers can't keep up with the flow of words. I know this is my right place because I feel really connected to nature and life. This is where I find myself most inspired just being in the moment, which I need as a writer.

Ideally, I'd live in a place that inspires me like this every day. Sometimes life prevents this. Family, financial restrictions, work, and other life circumstances can get in the way of living in our ideal place. Instead, we may need to find time to slip away to this right place when we can.

When I need to write and I'm unable to slip off to an apartment for a few days, I take my chair and pop-up table down to the beach or park and write from there. It might not be my perfect place, but it still feels good.

The more we love where we are, the better we feel. It gives us a greater sense of gratitude and happiness. We may not be clear about our direction or who we are, but we feel more aligned with being in the now. When our heart sings, so does our life and relationships. Think about how good you feel when you watch a sunset from a beautiful beach, or you look off into the distance from the peak of a mountain. This feel-good energy helps us resonate within our G centre and helps us attract the things we want and love in our life.

If you feel stuck in a situation, it could be because you're in the wrong place with the wrong people. Finding the right place for you can help alleviate feeling stuck and will allow you to grow and move in a direction that is more aligned with your authentic self.

COACHING TIPS

1. HOME SWEET HOME - IF HOME DOESN'T FEEL SWEET, CHANGE IT

Home should be your sanctuary. At the very least, a room or space within your home should feel this way. If your home doesn't feel good to spend time in, it's time to make some changes. This means you may need to find somewhere completely new to live. Feeling good in your home space is essential.

If you're a country girl at heart, but currently living in the city, either move back to the country or find a home that feels like a country home and aligns with what feels good for you. If you're sharing a cramped house with a bunch of people who have no sense of personal space, it is unlikely you'll feel good for very long as a Reflector in this space. In these circumstances, if moving is an option, take it.

If you simply can't change where you live, change what you can within your home. Ideas to help your home feel better:

- Learn Feng-Shui and make the necessary changes.
- Change or reposition the furniture.
- Add elements that make you happy such as plants, photos, candles, flowers, smells, or other decorations.
- Adopt a pet – this may help you enjoy being home more.
- Employ a cleaner if you struggle with keeping it clean. A clean home can really help us feel good.
- Add extra light. Warm lighting or light fixtures such as string lights can help increase the ambience of your home

making it cozier and more appealing. Even adding an extra window can help let in more natural light.

- Change at least one place in your home so that if feels good to spend time in. Your bedroom, your office, the garden, or even the kitchen can be improved so they feel good to you. Find at least one space within your home that you can call your sanctuary.

2. LOVE WHERE YOU WORK OR CHANGE IT

Most people spend nearly half their waking life at work. For this reason, it's just as important for Reflectors to ensure the workplace feels good to work in.

When you loathe going to work because it doesn't feel good to be there, it may be time to find another job. A toxic workplace can be detrimental to a Reflector's health. Doing the right work is also important, but for now, we're referring to how you feel within the workplace.

If changing where you work isn't an option, change what you can within your workplace so that it feels better:

- Ask to move to a different physical work location. Perhaps, you can change desks, floor levels, or move to a different work site.
- Spruce up your desk or workspace by getting rid of clutter and by adding photos, plants, lamps, flowers, smells, or other decorations you love.
- Give yourself a comfortable place to sit by adding cushions, getting a padded chair, or investing in a foot stool so you can work more comfortably.
- Reinvent your workspace by changing your desk, repositioning furniture, and anything else you can do to create a space that feels better for you to work in.

- Get out of the office every day. Give yourself breaks during your workday to visit places that feel good. Visit your favourite café, take a walk in the park, or just get outside and bask in the sun. The key here is to find time to give yourself a break from your work environment and to find pockets of time that allow you to feel great in places you love.

3. CHOOSE PLACES AND SPACES THAT FEEL GOOD

Whenever you have a choice, choose to spend time in places that feel good. When you go out to eat, choose a restaurant that you enjoy sitting in. When you go on holiday, choose places that allow you to feel good and relaxed to maximise your enjoyment while you're there. When you go out for a walk, choose a path that feels good to walk down if you have options. Choosing places that feel good will allow you to have more pleasant experiences in these places.

4. COMMUNICATE YOUR NEEDS

If you go somewhere and end up in a seat that doesn't feel good, don't be afraid to ask someone with a defined G centre to swap their seat with you. This typically won't bother a person with a defined G centre as much as it will affect you. Don't put up with being somewhere that doesn't feel good unless you have no other choice.

Have an open conversation about your need to be in the right place with the people you spend the most time with. This can make life easier for you. When these people understand how important this is for you, that won't question your request to, for example, change seats in a restaurant or sleep on a certain side of the bed. With awareness, these people can help accommodate your needs and proactively ensure you have input into choosing the places you spend time together.

Communicating these needs will also prevent people from thinking you've gone a little bit mad when they find you rearranging furniture in the middle of the night so you can sleep better.

5. SPEND TIME WITH PEOPLE WHO FEEL GOOD

A Reflector's identity and direction is greatly impacted by the people in our life. This is why it's important to remove people from your life who don't feel good to be around. If you allow yourself to spend too much time with people who don't have a healthy sense of self or life direction, they can negatively influence your own sense of self.

Some people will always be in your life. If you can't remove these people completely:

- Change how much time you spend with them.
- Prepare and protect yourself emotionally and energetically before spending time with them.
- Find other strategies to cope when you're with these people. You could ask someone else to join you every time you see this person. You may only choose to see them in an environment that positively impacts you both, such as in a social setting.
- Understand how they impact you and do all you can to discharge their energy when you leave so they don't impact the rest of your day.

To enhance these positive influences on your identity and life direction, spend more time with people who feel good to be around. These people help you feel good inside and will lift you up spiritually when you're in their presence.

THE CHALLENGE
OF BECOMING A
HUMAN BAROMETER

*A ship in harbor is safe, but that is
not what ships are built for.*
                    - John A. Shedd

REFLECTORS ARE HERE FOR OTHER PEOPLE.
Like a canary in a coalmine, we are here to reflect back
the health of our community. Canaries were once used in
coalmines to provide the miners with an early warning system.
The miners would know when the gas levels in the mine were
becoming hazardous because the canaries would die before the
gas reached toxic levels and killed the miners. The canaries
were far more sensitive to the environment than the miners.
The canaries provided an early warning signal so the miners
could make changes to the way they were working and save
their own lives.

Like these canaries, Reflectors are able to sense what is
happening within our environment before everyone else.
Through our sensitive connection to the environment, we can
signal to our community how healthy things are and provide an

early warning signal when our community is becoming toxic and unhealthy to ensure humanity carries on in the healthiest direction.

To fulfil our role as barometers, we must signal to our community when they have gone off track. We must let them know when things become so toxic that their lives are in danger. We need to be the signpost that tells them when they need to make changes before the toxicity consumes them. We exist as both a warning signal and a guiding light. We can let people know when they have gone off track and when they are headed in the right direction.

We cannot sample and reflect back to our community by sitting in our loungerooms. We must be active participants within our community and the world if we are to sample the health of these environments. When we don't spend enough time out in our community so we can play our part, we are unable to fulfil our Reflector role and we are without purpose.

It is also more difficult to understand the health of the world around us when we have nothing else to compare it to. We need to be able to distinguish between our own energy, the energy of others, the energy of our community, and comparatively, the energy of other communities, so we can truly be the human barometer we are designed to be.

SOLUTION – EXPLORE FOR PERSPECTIVE

The more we experience in life, the wiser we become about ourselves and the world around us. The more we see, hear, and experience, the more wisdom we gain and the more we can step into our role as Reflectors. The more we sample, the better equipped we are at distinguishing between our own energy, thoughts, and feelings and those we have absorbed from other people. This also gives us the innate ability to be a human barometer recognising the true health of our community.

If we want to reflect back the health and wellbeing of our community, we need to spend time within our community. If we want to understand how our community is performing compared to other communities, we need to visit other communities so we can draw comparisons. It is hard to be wise and understand our observations when we have nothing to compare them to.

If I spent my life trapped in a cave underground only ever knowing and sampling the energy of the people who lived in the cave, this is all I would know. Without experiencing any other place or people, I would only be able to make observations in the context of the cave. If, one day, I was no longer trapped in the cave and I saw the outside world for the first time, the observations about my cave experience would be very different. Now I would be contextually comparing my cave experiences to those of the outside world.

Explore as many different things, people, and places as possible. The more you sample, the more you learn. Visiting other communities and cultures to sample the energy of people who are different from those in our local community is an incredibly empowering experience for Reflectors. Just like sampling food from different cultures expands our experience of taste, sampling energies from other cultures expands our experience of the world and those within it. We no longer see the world purely through the eyes of our local community. Instead, we experience and sample life through the global community. Life becomes easier to navigate. We gain a clearer perspective of the world around us. We step more fully into our role as Reflectors.

Travel helps Reflectors become wise. Spending time with different people and trying different things all contribute to our wisdom. The more diverse energies we sample, the more enlightened we become about ourselves and our own communities. We can see and feel things from multiple viewpoints, seeing both the bigger picture and the more granular detail at the local level. The more we sample, the more effectively we can play our part as a wise observer of the world.

Whenever you can, I urge you to try new things. Try different types of work, hobbies, relationships, and friends. This is all perspective building. It is so much fun sampling the vastly different ways of living, people, and places. Go! Explore everything!

COACHING TIPS

1. GET TO KNOW DIFFERENT PEOPLE

As Reflectors, we sample energy and naturally adapt ourselves to the person or people we are with. This gives us the opportunity to experience the world through many different lenses. Don't just spend time with people who are similar to yourself. Get to know people who are different so you can experience the extremes in different energies, thoughts, and feelings. Not only does this make us wise about people, it also helps us to become wise about what feels right for us.

2. TRY DIFFERENT TYPES OF WORK

Rather than play it safe in a job you are comfortable doing, explore other types of work to really get an understanding of how different work makes you feel. As Reflectors, we tend to get bored easily doing the same thing. A change in work keeps things interesting and gives us a broader experience of work. Do this temporarily if you must. This can be as simple as taking on a weekend job or night work for a short time. You can try working as a bartender, an English as a second language teacher, a volunteer, or something that is vastly different from your usual work. Naturally, only engage in work you feel energetically capable of doing.

Maybe, after spending your weekends volunteering at a dog shelter, you may discover that working with animals is what brings you the most joy. This could change the course of your career and life, and you'll finally be on a path that feels right for you.

These experiences also give us insight into the world of work, including the different types of work, the people who work within them, and the varying work tasks. These experiences provide us with further wisdom about the world around us and the work we personally enjoy doing.

If you don't try it out, you'll never know. You may even discover, like I did, that doing different work every few years is what feels best as a vocation, and this becomes your right path. It's all about trying it out, so you can learn from the experience and discover what feels most aligned for you. Regardless of whether you love or hate this work, you'll observe and learn a lot as a Reflector, and this will help you fulfil your role as a wise observer.

3. EXPLORE SEX AND RELATIONSHIPS

Reflectors like consistent energy around us. We have an open Spleen centre which means we can easily fall into relationships early in life and stay in those relationships even if they're not great for us. Without experiencing other people in a relationship context, it is hard to know if the relationship we are in is the best relationship for us. We don't know what we don't know.

It is, therefore, advantageous to experiment with different types of partners before we settle down with just one. Through experimentation and dating lots of different types of people, we get a better sense of what type of relationship feels right for us and the type of person that brings out the best in us. After all, this will be the person we reflect back the most once we're living with them.

Our open Sacral centre makes us exploratory when it comes to sex. We can enjoy sex in many different ways unlike our Generator friends who have a consistent way of expressing their sexuality. This means we can have vastly different sexual experiences based on the person we engage in sex with. Allowing ourselves to experience different sexual partners helps us to understand what feels right for us and gives us a greater perspective and understanding about sexual relationships and the various sexual experiences that are available to us.

4. TRAVEL WHEREVER YOU CAN

Travel allows us to experience many different ways of living away from the familiarity of our own backyard. If you can, visit other countries and cultures including a variety of socio-economic regions. Travel to different types of environments, such as cities, rural areas, and rainforests. Spend time interacting with and observing people within these different places to sample their energy, thoughts, and feelings. Observe the way they live and how this differs from your current life experiences.

a) Start local

If the thought of travel scares you or you don't have the funds to travel far, start by travelling locally. Find a way to interact with people you wouldn't normally interact with in places you normally wouldn't go. If you live in a city, get out into the country and spend time around people who aren't from the city. See how this feels. Become conscious of how you feel in each place and around different types of people. This will help you start to build perspective.

b) Travel to places that aren't on your bucket list

Travelling to places you have a strong desire to visit has its benefits. But, travelling somewhere that isn't on your 'must go' list is usually a place that can bring you a lot of wisdom, energetically.

I had no desire to go to Dubai. A huge city in a desert really never appealed to me. In fact, I think I was a bit repelled by what it represented. Then, someone I was in love with moved there and invited me to join him. I went, despite how I felt about the place, for reasons of the heart. Surprisingly, my experience of living in Dubai for two years was energetically amazing. I experienced many different cultures, people, and places while there. I learned a lot about myself and other people. I also cultivated a greater appreciation of my hometown because I was able to contextualise it within a global perspective.

Travelling to places outside of your comfort zone can be truly rewarding. The more you sample energetically, the more you build perspective and wisdom.

c) Travel often

Travelling often, whether it's locally or internationally, is the key to ensuring you don't lose sight of what's important and what may be impacting you energetically on a daily basis. It can also top up your energetic 'feel good' tank and help you discharge energies that no longer serve you. The more places you see and the more people you meet, the greater your wisdom and perspective will be.

The more we experience, the more we get to know our true selves. The more we know our selves, the more successfully we can play our part as Reflectors. We can then tune into the health of our communities and provide an early warning signal to help humanity move forward in the right direction.

The Challenge of
Living With Fear

*Every time you are tempted to react in the
same old way, ask if you want to be a prisoner
of the past or a pioneer of the future.*
— Deepak Chopra

THE SPLEEN IS THE ENERGY CENTRE for intuition,
health, survival, and time. It is very time-specific, and it
affects our direct reactive response in the moment. Because this
centre is about in the moment responses, it is also where fear
lives in the chart.

When we feel threatened, this centre enables our fight or
flight response in the moment to ensure our survival. When
we respond to a life-threatening event by running away, this
response literally saves our life. Unfortunately, the Spleen
centre can cause us to react in the same way to any threat, even
if it's not actually life threatening.

If we have defined gates in the Spleen centre, it means
we are vulnerable to the fears of the spleen. When we feel
threatened in the moment, if we let the fears of the Spleen take
over, we can become paralyzed with fear. Today we respond to

stress in a similar way to survival, even when our lives aren't under threat.

Depending on our definition within the gates of the Spleen, we can become fearful of many things. We can fear being inadequate. We can fear not being good enough. We can fear the future or the past. We can even fear failing or fear that life has no meaning. When we are susceptible to these fears and we don't learn to manage them, we can stay stuck in fear and unable to progress in life to fulfil our roles as Reflectors.

I have the gate 48 defined in my chart, which gives me a fear of inadequacy. I've had many losses in my life because I let this fear gate get the better of me. I quit playing the piano at 18 because my boyfriend at the time also played the piano. He was so good that I felt completely inadequate in comparison to him, so I quit and never played again.

When I was younger, I dated an amazing guy I worked with who I thought was completely out of my league. I thought he didn't have any serious intentions with me because of this. At a work party, I casually kissed another guy and he witnessed. Years later, he told me that that moment broke his heart. I was crushed. I had no idea he felt that way, and I missed out on a relationship with someone really special because of my own inadequacy fears.

With our open Spleen centre, we also easily absorb and amplify the fears of other people. Fear can completely overcome us if we let it. We can have a hard time managing fear because of this. Overcoming the fears of the Spleen is vital for Reflectors to live a happy and healthy life.

SOLUTION – TUNE INTO
YOUR INTUITION

─────────── ▢ ───────────

As the centre for instinct in the moment, the Spleen centre is where our intuition comes from. It's important that we pay attention to the intuitive urges we receive within our bodies; the in-the-moment instinctive pulse to do something or not. We don't receive intuition in a consistent way, so there are many ways it shows up for us. Intuition can come as gut feelings, guiding voices, dreams, visions, etc. Our open Spleen centre delivers these messages to us, but we tend to doubt them because of their inconsistent delivery.

Intuition plays an important role because it helps with our survival. We must acknowledge the messages of our Spleen, including intuitive messages of fear. When you're walking somewhere late at night and a little voice in your head says, "don't go down that alleyway." Or, when you get a sinking feeling in your gut as you approach the alleyway, this is a fear-based survival message from your Spleen centre. These are intuitive messages that our Spleen gives us in the moment. We need to listen to them in that moment, otherwise they are no longer useful. Hindsight is a great thing, but it's useless wishing you'd listened to that voice in your head two hours after you've been mugged walking down a dark alley. These instinctive messages are timebound and are for that moment only.

When you find yourself gripped with fear over something, ask yourself if this a reasonable response. Is my fear justified by the outcome? Some fears have a useful place in our lives. They provide us with the instinctive hesitation to walk down that dark alleyway and they can save our lives, but often our fears are unsubstantiated.

If you're in a dangerous part of town in the middle of the night and there is no one else around, it is probably wise to listen to this intuitive voice. However, if the voice of fear arises in a non-life-threatening situation, notice the message but don't necessarily follow through on actioning it.

For example, we may develop a fear of going out in public. Unless we're living in a war zone, or there is some other life-threatening reason to stay inside, pushing through the fear and going out where there are other people won't kill you.

All fears of the Spleen are in-the-moment fears. Whether the fear is something that comes from within us or it is a fear we absorb and amplify from someone else, if we push through the fear (feel the fear and do it anyway), the fear soon dissipates. The Spleen centre is our mastery centre. If we manage to push through these in-the-moment fears, we often find they lead us to mastering something and achieving more than we imagined.

With the fear of inadequacy gate defined in my Spleen centre, I often think I'm not quite good enough or I don't know enough to take on something new. I overcompensate by being extremely prepared and spending all my time getting as much information and detail about something as I can before I take on a new endeavour. I've turned down job opportunities because I thought I didn't have enough experience or knowledge while I watched other people with less experience and knowledge acquire these jobs.

One day, I applied for a job I thought I was adequately skilled for. At the group job interview session, I soon learned that I was the least experienced person who applied. When this dawned on me halfway through the interview, I was too embarrassed to walk out so I stuck around.

I did the best I could and just when I thought the interview was over, the interviewer asked us to each stand up and talk on the spot about something important to establish if we could think on our feet. This was something I was good at. I left the interview still believing the role was definitely not mine, but at least I'd finished the interview on a high.

When they called me the next day to tell me I'd made it through to the next round of interviews, I was shocked. The whole interview process took three weeks. They were looking for a highly-skilled person, but they were also looking for a certain X factor. Self-aware about my lack of experience, I improvised my way through the rest of the interview sessions. I felt the fear and did it anyway since I'd already made it this far. When I was offered the job over all other candidates, I was a changed person. I realized that all those fears I had harboured about my inadequacies for so many years had been unwarranted.

Since then, when I sense that something I want to achieve is slightly out of my comfort zone, and I sense a feeling of inadequacy taking over, I push on anyway just to see how far I can get. Most of the time, I land on my feet. I not only get through the fear, but I excel. I now seek out these opportunities where I can push myself beyond these fears. I love the feeling of exhilaration and achievement I get when I land on the other side of the fear still in one piece. It's absolutely worth that scary leap. Pushing through these fears is what allows us to achieve mastery in something.

When we learn to feel the fear and do it anyway, we gain a real sense of achievement. If you've ever jumped out of a plane skydiving, you'll understand what I mean. Those moments before the jump can be overwhelming with fearful thoughts. However, once you manage to push through the fear and jump, a few seconds later you get an amazing rush as you gracefully float through the sky.

For those who aren't so keen on heights, think of the first time you ever kissed someone. The lead up to that kiss was completely unnerving. You were thinking, what if I don't know how to kiss properly, what if they don't really like me, or what if it tastes bad. The moment after you took that first kiss, whether it was a good one or not, you felt a sense of achievement. You at least got that first kiss out of the way. Perhaps it was even better than you imagined.

When you have an in-the-moment fear response, determine the severity of the outcome and act accordingly. Don't become a victim to the fears of your Spleen. Tune in to how fear plays out in your life. If you find yourself unjustifiably paralysed by the fears of the Spleen centre, it's time to stop letting it effect your ability to live a full and healthy life.

COACHING TIPS

1. PAY ATTENTION TO YOUR IN-THE-MOMENT INTUITION

We continually receive intuitive messages. These messages are timebound and need to be attended to in the moment. Pay attention to these messages and notice what they are telling you. Messages can come from many different sources. You may receive messages in your gut, voices in your head, signs, or other intuitive vehicles. Notice when you receive an intuitive message and listen to what it has to say.

2. DETERMINE THE VALUE OF THE MESSAGE AND ACT ACCORDINGLY

Once you receive an intuitive message, determine if this is something you should pay attention to or not. If the message is fear-based, consider whether the fear is justified.

For example, if you are about to go on a first date and you get a fearful intuitive message that tells you not to go, determine if this is fear is founded. Once you determine that your fear is unjustifiable and is founded on one previous bad dating experience, this can help you feel the fear and do it anyway. The date isn't actually going to kill you (we hope!).

3. PUSH THROUGH THE FEAR

When you have a fear response that isn't justified, push through the fear and do it anyway. If your fear impulse tells you you're not yet ready to start a new job, or you're not good enough for a new partner, acknowledge the fear and then let it pass. Push through the fear and take on the new job or partner anyway.

You'll be surprised how good it feels once you push past this fear. It's liberating and thrilling when you achieve something you originally thought you couldn't. Don't ever let fear stop you from doing something. Fear only gets in the way of fulfilling your true potential.

THE CHALLENGE OF LACK OF ENERGY

March to the beat of your own drum.
- Henry David Thoreau

R EFLECTORS HAVE AN OPEN SACRAL CENTRE. This means we don't have access to consistent life force and workforce energy, or the energy for doing.

Without access to consistent sustainable energy, Reflectors can find repetitive everyday tasks quite challenging. We usually prefer to do anything over daily household chores, such as cleaning. Many people don't enjoy chores, but Reflectors really struggle with the mundane and repetitiveness of these tasks and they sap our energy in a way that isn't sustainable.

Reflectors are much more interested in using this limited energy for more novel and diverse activities that aren't mindless and energetically draining. Without consistent energy, our behaviors can be judged unfairly by people who have their Sacral centre defined and have access to this sustainable energy source. As children and sometimes into adulthood, this lack of energy is often perceived by others as laziness.

I can't tell you the number of times I was in trouble for not keeping my room clean or for not doing kitchen-related chores as a child. I abhorred them. I still can't stand the monotony of these chores today. I may find the energy to do them one day, but then the next day, the chores need doing again. I can't see the point of wasting valuable time and energy doing something that will only need doing again tomorrow.

As a child, I preferred to spend my time and focus on learning new things, writing plays, and doing more novel tasks such as working out how to connect the new DVD player for my Dad who couldn't be bothered reading through the instruction manual.

Even today, I'd prefer to paint the house than do the dishes. Sure, I probably don't have the energy to complete the painting job, but I'm much more motivated to get into a job like this than to do something like washing dishes. Luckily, I have an amazing husband who doesn't mind washing the dishes in exchange for me doing more mentally draining tasks.

Our lack of energy is often greatly misunderstood. We can be unfairly judged by others because of this, and we can be very hard on ourselves. This can cause us to push to prove ourselves with energy we don't really have, eventually burning ourselves out.

Solution – Understand Your Energy Needs

Understand how your open Sacral centre affects you energetically. Accept that you don't have consistent sustainable energy and that you're designed differently from 70% of other people. Be more forgiving of yourself and the expectations you put on yourself trying to keep up with other people. Know that you're not lazy. Stop identifying yourself with other people's judgements. Most people are very different than you.

If people think you're lazy, let them. You know that your avoidance of mundane tasks is driven by something very different than a lack of motivation and laziness. Stop believing the labels that other people put on you and you put on yourself.

When someone accuses you of being lazy, you can arm yourself with knowledge about the way your energy works and communicate this with your accuser.

When I explained to my husband how I felt about doing routine daily chores and how my energy works as a Reflector, he said he'd gladly take some of these chores off my hands when he could. As a Generator, he has the energy to take on more of the mundane and energy-draining chores while I focus on the chores that are less tedious and strenuous.

At first, I felt guilty about this. He seemed to be contributing more than me physically around the house. Then, I realised that I contribute to our relationship by giving him a lot of my support and mental capacity. I help him in so many ways that aren't physical but are equally important. I help him see what is right for him. I mirror back the state of his health and keep him on a healthy life path. I ensure his needs are met because I sense what he needs.

I no longer feel guilty when he does the dishes more than I do. I always do what I can around the house, but I give him something he didn't have before he met me. I give him the ability to be truly seen, accepted, and allowed to be himself. I continually support him in this capacity.

Regardless of what other people say, you are not lazy. When it's appropriate, communicate your energy preservation needs with other people. Do what you can to negotiate a life that accommodates these needs. You are not being lazy when you need to rest more than other people. You are not lazy when you don't have the energy to sustain physically draining activities the way other people can. You are merely preserving energy so you can utilize your gifts in a more productive way.

COACHING TIPS

1. UNDERSTAND YOUR LACK OF ENERGY

Recognise that your lack of desire to do tedious tasks is not laziness but a way for you to conserve your limited energy reserves. You can borrow the Sacral centre energy from Generators to get some things done but understand this is only for short periods of time and this is not sustainable. When you must draw on your energetic resources, you want your energy to be utilised in the most productive and effective way possible. Use your energy wisely. Don't judge yourself for your inability to keep doing and doing.

2. TELL PEOPLE ABOUT YOUR ENERGY CONSERVATION NEEDS

When possible, tell people about your need to conserve energy and why you may appear 'lazy' so they can understand and even support you in following your unique path.

If you don't feel comfortable telling them about what it means to be a Reflector, find another way to negotiate tasks with other people to meet your energetic needs. Swap tasks with someone. Take tasks that you don't mind doing and give tasks that really deplete you to someone else.

This applies not only to domestic chores but also work chores. If your job has some component of regular tasks that really tax your energy as a Reflector, try to swap these tasks with someone else.

I enjoy organising things - from organising events to organising files on a computer. Many of my colleagues hate this type of work. I often take on these tasks for them and hand over the tasks that I find more taxing, such as coordinating tasks and running errands.

By unloading some of these regular tedious tasks, you can use your energy for things that really matter to you and which are less draining. If you can pay someone to do these tasks for you, for example by getting a cleaner, do it! Remember you are NOT lazy, regardless of what other people may think. You are just a very good energy conservationist!

THE CHALLENGE
OF LINEAR TIME

*All we have to decide is what to do with
the time that is given to us.*
- J.R.R. Tolkien

REFLECTORS HAVE A TENDENCY to run late. This
is because we often struggle with time. With our open
Spleen centre, we have a very fluid connection to the time
space continuum. We tend to get lost in the moment and lose
track of time. We don't have a strong connection to linear time
and minutes can sometimes seem like hours, or the other way
around. This means we can miss our time commitments if
we aren't cautiously clock watching. To deal with this lack of
timeliness, we can over-compensate by being extremely early
to our time commitments or have lots of mechanisms in place,
such as alarms, to ensure we keep track of time and we aren't
late.

Other people, especially people with a defined Spleen
centre, don't necessarily understand this. They may see
Reflectors as unorganised and late or forgetful. The beauty of
being so in the moment as a Reflector is that we can take a
deep dive into something and really explore whatever we are

engaged in at that moment. It's just that we don't have an innate internal awareness of how long things are taking or when it's time to do something else.

I can't recall a single occasion when I've been late because I was being lazy or irresponsible. It is nearly always because I've been so engaged in whatever else I'm doing, believing I can fit it all in, that time just slips away from me and I'm suddenly running late. No matter how hard I try, I just can't manage to get on top of time.

I enjoy cooking when I have the time to do it at my own pace and when I'm not too tired. I'm reasonably capable of creating a delicious meal. When I have multiple dishes cooking in the kitchen in preparation for a meal, it's almost a guarantee that I'll burn or overcook something. No matter how much I try to multi-task and cook different elements of a meal at once, I inevitably forget about something because I'm deeply focused on another part of the meal.

Even if I have only one thing cooking on the stove and I sit down at the table to do some work on my laptop, there is a very good chance that I'll burn the meal if I don't set an alarm. I become so ingrained in the thing I am doing at that moment that I forget about everything else – including dinner cooking on the stove. I have to set alarms now to ensure I don't burn food. Otherwise, I just stand there in the kitchen watching dinner cook so I don't forget about it, but usually this is far too mundane for me to do for too long.

SOLUTION – MANAGE YOUR TIME

With awareness about your lack of timeliness, you can put strategies in place to manage this. You can set alarms or reminders to help yourself stay on track.

My kitchen clock, which is the clock I look at the most, is set 10 to 15 minutes fast. Even though I know I've set it this way, it still helps me to be on time because I never know exactly how fast it is. I usually work on the notion that it's less ahead of time than it really is.

Meeting time obligations can be very stressful for a Reflector. This includes going to work. Starting at a specific time every day can be quite daunting no matter how hard we try to get there on time.

When the pressure of trying to be on time was causing me undue stress, I asked my employer if I could have a more flexible start time. I requested to start between 8:30 a.m. and 9:30 a.m. each day and then work my eight hours accordingly. I explained that I had a busy morning schedule and I was getting to work feeling stressed out by trying to get everything done in order to make it into the office by a specific minute. They were more than agreeable with this, and it took the pressure off me having to be in the office on the dot at 8:30 a.m. Many organisations say they offer flexible work arrangements these days, so it's worthwhile to ask about this if you believe it will help you.

Where possible, don't set specific start times. If you're meeting a friend for coffee, organise an approximate time and tell her you'll text her when you're leaving the house. This way, she doesn't have to wait for you and you don't have to worry about being there on the dot.

When this isn't possible, at least allow yourself to be free of time restrictions on the weekends. People will understand if you let them know why this is important to you. Set an alarm for the commitments that you must be on time for and prepare accordingly. For everything else, give yourself the freedom to work with flexible timing so you reduce this stress in your life and go with your own flow more, free of linear time restrictions.

COACHING TIPS

1. SET ALARMS AND REMINDERS TO HELP WITH TIMELINESS

When being on time is important, set up whatever tactics you can to avoid being late. Being late is usually not an option for appointments and meetings, and it can be frowned on by others. When you can't negotiate a more flexible start time, set alarms, reminders, or whatever methods you can employ to ensure you get to these things on time. Even change the clocks in your house if this helps – and avoid looking at the real time on your phone.

Reminder setting is also useful when you're engaged in activities that require you to watch the time carefully, such as when you're cooking. If you must cook complex recipes or there's a chance of burning your food, stand over it and watch it cook so you're fully engaged and not distracted. Alternatively, set an alarm to ensure you don't forget about that lovely cake you laboured over now cooking in the oven.

2. BE REALISTIC ABOUT HOW MUCH YOU WILL ACHIEVE

We often overestimate the amount of time we have to do activities and how much we can get done in a day. In an ideal world, we can achieve many things, but often life gets in the way of achieving these ideals.

During work hours, we may think we can fit in six appointments or we can complete a report. However, we often underestimate how long something will take. Life typically gets in the way of meeting our own deadlines and we exhaust ourselves trying to achieve them. Our computer crashes and we spend an hour fixing it. Someone calls and needs some urgent help with something. Buying lunch takes longer than it should. Travelling between appointments involves worse traffic than usual. It takes us more time to get into the flow of writing a document than we thought it would.

There are many reasons why we typically don't get as much done as we think we can. We aren't Manifesting Generators. We can't successfully juggle multiple things at once, so stop putting unrealistic expectations and pressure on yourself.

Finally, be realistic about what is achievable given your unsustainable energy source. Look back at how much you typically achieve in a day or a week when you plan your schedule and be realistic about how much you will actually get done. Don't overbook yourself. This will not only contribute to your inability to be on time, it will cause you stress, further taxing your limited energy supplies.

PART TWO

Keep Healthy

A S NON-SACRAL BEINGS, Reflectors will easily burn out. We are vulnerable to health issues due to our complete openness. Without sustainable lifeforce energy, we need to protect our health and ensure we live long, healthy lives. Life can be challenging for Reflectors when we don't listen to our internal guidance system, which tells us when we're in danger of burning ourselves out.

This section has three main challenges:

- Burn out
- Sleep
- Sensitive Immune System

Each chapter within this section is dedicated to exploring one of these challenges and provides tips for living a healthy life as a Reflector.

The Challenge
of Burn Out

Respect your body when it's asking for a break.
Respect your mind when it's seeking rest. Honor
yourself when you need a moment for yourself.
- Unknown

UNLIKE MANY OF OUR FRIENDS, colleagues, and family, Reflectors don't have the energy to keep going and going like the Energizer Bunny. We simply don't have access to the sustainable work force and life force sacral energy that 70% of people are born with, like Generator types.

This means we don't have the same ability to work hard all day through the daily grind, go to sleep, and then get up and do it all over again day after day. We may be able to do this for short periods of time, but when we attempt to push ourselves energetically over longer periods, we risk burning ourselves out completely.

Generator types can have an exhausting couple of days and still manage to pick themselves up, dust themselves off, and then go back and do it all over again. Reflectors are simply not made this way. Our energy is not sustainable. Pushing ourselves to use energy that we just don't have has serious consequences to our health.

If we don't pay attention to our need for rest and restoration when we're young, and we continue to push ourselves like our Generator friends, we risk burning out completely after 40 years of age. Once we're burnt out, it becomes harder to find even the short bursts of energy that we once relied on to keep up with everyone else. Instead, we may struggle to find the motivation and energy we need to sustain ourselves. After this age, working and taking care of our families can seem like momentous tasks for Reflectors.

When I was in my 20s, I completed three degrees while working mostly full-time. I also managed to have a great social life and live with other people. I spent those years living off the energetic fumes of other people's sacral energy. I thought I was invincible and often felt like the most energetic person I knew.

This soon wore off when I entered into my 30s. As I crawled closer to 40, the harder it became to keep up with everyone else. This didn't stop me from trying. I kept going, pushing myself with borrowed energy, assuming that I would always have the same access to the energy I had in my younger years. Then, things started to change within me.

The closer I crept toward 40, the more I became unwell. I developed several food and chemical intolerances and my digestive system stopped functioning properly. But, I kept going. I didn't understand what was wrong with me. I had a healthier diet than ever before, and I certainly wasn't working any harder. In fact, work was easier given that I no longer had to work and study at the same time. Every doctor I visited told me it was due to stress. They told me I needed to reduce the stress in my life.

Even though I didn't feel particularly stressed, I removed more and more things that were possibly causing me stress. I reduced my work hours until I was working only three days a week. I moved home to a location closer to work, so my travel time was reduced. I took ridiculous amounts of vitamins and drank green smoothies every day made with nothing but green vegetables. I even removed people from my life who weren't healthy for me.

Each year, I reduced my stressors more and more until I only worked part time from home, slept as much as I needed, ate only healthy home cooked meals, hardly did anything much - and still my body was tired and I couldn't find the energy to get up and go like I used to. I still had the same pains, intolerances, and health conditions that were apparently due to stress. Yet, I had barely any stress left in my life. I couldn't have lived more simply unless I stayed bed bound.

It was then that I realized that I had burned myself out and my body simply didn't have the energy to fully restore itself. I'd spent too much of my life living on borrowed energy and I was left with a deficit.

If only I had found out earlier that I was a Reflector. I may have stopped pushing with energy I didn't really have. I may have taken more time to be a chilled person when I was younger instead of a high achiever who was jet-setting all over the world for work. I may not have burned out my digestive system, my immune system, my ovaries, and my brain.

Hindsight is a wonderful thing. But, I refuse to dwell on regrets. I've learned the hard way what can happen to a Reflector's health when we push too hard in life. My role is now to warn others about what can happen if we don't take time to properly rest and restore ourselves. I could be a lot worse. I am grateful that my health issues are not critical and are manageable. I would prefer not to suffer with them every day, but I am grateful of the teachings and wisdom they have granted me.

Having an open Sacral centre causes Reflectors to have a hard time knowing when enough is enough. When we borrow this motor energy, it is very easy for us to keep going, unaware of how this effects our bodies until it's too late and the damage is done.

Solution – Rest, Restore, and Rejuvenate

Understand the impact of stress on your body. Reflectors must rest, restore, and rejuvenate. This is easier said than done - I know! We need to find regular time in our daily lives to restore ourselves. Rest can be anything from a few minutes between meetings to a regular long weekend at the beach.

When we rest, it needs to be complete rest. This means we need to find regular time when we do absolutely nothing. Most of us have preferred ways we like to rest. The activity we do to rest isn't important as long as it allows us to completely rest our mind and body. Activities such as yin yoga, meditation, and other mindfulness activities are all good ways to switch off our constantly-chattering mind and our internal pressure to do and think. Whatever restful activity you choose, make sure that it allows you to just be with yourself.

Some sports can be good to help you mentally rest, but they need to be performed alone and they can't be too physically intense. Team sports don't give you the alone time you need away from other people's energy and therefore aren't truly restful. Team sports can be really beneficial, so don't give them up if you play in a team. Just don't count team sports as a restful and restorative activity.

Some physical activity can be restorative. Walking and even light jogging are beneficial. High intensity activities, however, should not be classed as part of your rest and restoration routine. They may play an important role in your life, but they won't necessarily give you the restoration that you need. They can also deplete you further if they're too exhausting.

Find as many opportunities as possible to be in the moment and just rest. These restful moments will rejuvenate and restore you by allowing you to discharge the energy you pick up during the day from other people. It also gives you a chance to rest your mind and focus on what Reflectors are truly here to do – to just be.

Regular periods of rest can include a hot bath each night on your own while reading a book or just staring into space. You may like to spend the weekend sleeping in alone or taking the dog to the beach and just sitting for a while with your feet in the ocean.

When you feel yourself pushing – pushing on, pushing through something, or pushing yourself, this is the time when you need to stop and rest. This is the time when you do the most damage by not stopping and listening to your body. We have an open Spleen centre. This means we have a sensitive immune system that knows when we're pushing ourselves too far. We need to pay attention to this awareness system. It can save us from our open Root centre that often pushes us to finish something so we can be free, as well as our open Sacral centre that doesn't know when enough is enough.

Even while writing this book, I experienced the result of pushing too hard. Toward the end of the writing process, when I needed to have the final draft finished by the end of a particular week, I locked myself away in a hotel room for two solid days wearing the keys on my laptop down with my intense typing. I felt myself drained and my sinuses indicated a cold was looming, but I was determined to soldier on. I kept pushing to get it done.

By the time I checked out of that hotel, I was a mess. I hadn't finished the final draft despite my best efforts, and I could barely hold myself up. When I got home, instead of getting back to writing, I had to take myself to bed. I was completely exhausted and unable to do any more writing for two days. Just walking to the kitchen to get food was an arduous task. This is a prime example of what can happen when we don't pay attention to our inner warning system and we push on with energy we just don't have. It's easy to ignore the warning signals and push on, but the consequences are never worth it.

Taking time out away from the busy daily grind of work and life activities is important for everyone. But for Reflectors, this is integral to maintaining a happy and healthy life. Unlike Generator types who can soldier on without much rest, Reflectors simply can't do this without serious consequences. Don't listen to other people who tell you to harden up when you say you need a break after a busy day or a long week. They likely don't understand your need for rest and assume that if they can get by without it, so can you. They are not you and they don't operate the same way energetically. Only you know when you need to rest. Don't risk your health to appease the judgements of other people or out of guilt trying to keep up with everyone else.

Take care of yourself and include a lot of rest in your routine. Don't push yourself to burn out. Your future self will thank you. Listen to your body and pay attention to your internal health warning system. It will tell you what you need and help you live a longer, healthier life. Give yourself the gift of rest whenever you need it.

COACHING TIPS

1. FIND YOUR PREFERRED WAY TO REST

There are plenty of options to choose from when it comes to rest and rejuvenation activities. The best restful activity for you to choose is the one that you enjoy doing the most. It should be an activity that is easy to fit into your life and it should allow you to feel completely rested. What's most important is that you find a way to rest that works for you. The activities you choose should ideally be done alone and allow you to be in the moment. These activities should take you away from over-thinking and over-doing and permit you to switch off your mind as much as possible.

There are literally thousands of restful activities to choose from. Ideas for restful activities include:

- Meditation
- Yin yoga
- Art and crafts
- Reading
- Walking
- Light jogging
- Spending time at the beach
- Picnic in the park
- Sleeping

2. SCHEDULE REGULAR RESTORATION ACTIVITIES

Consistent routines are highly beneficial for Reflectors. Scheduling in time for restful activities can help ensure you actually do them. You are better equipped to manage other demanding daily tasks when you have a regular restoration practice in place.

If you work full-time, find time in your day to take a break. With our fast-paced lifestyle, it's not unusual to skip lunch breaks altogether or eat lunch on the run. While this may be necessary at times, take a lunch break away from work and other people whenever you can. Try buying lunch once or twice a week so you leave your work environment during your lunch break. Maybe find somewhere to eat that is more relaxing than your desk. Using your break to go for a walk or to take a yoga class can also be restorative.

If taking a break during the day is too difficult, find time before or after work to do something restful. Take a walk, meditate, or have a bubble bath. Whatever restful activity you choose, make sure you do it. Even if the motivation to do something is hard to find, these activities will be rewarding once they are completed. Unlike stressful activities, they help you feel better. Just make sure you schedule these in at times that won't put you under more pressure. Trying to fit a yoga class in on a morning when you have a list of other activities to complete before work may ultimately make you more stressed. Timing is important. Ensure it isn't rushed and allows you to unwind properly.

If you spend the majority of your time around other people, make sure you find time to do something restful alone. This will allow you to discharge the energy you've picked up from other people during the day and it will rejuvenate your cells.

3. PAY ATTENTION TO YOUR INNER GUIDANCE SYSTEM

When you notice yourself pushing to get things done or to keep going, do whatever you can to stop and rest. You may find the energy to push through and complete something, but you will pay with your health later. This payment may be immediate. You may be physically drained for a day or two after this pushing period. While the effects may not show up immediately, if you keep existing like this, your health will eventually suffer. You may feel invincible now, but as you reach 40 and beyond, the damage you did to your body by pushing too much in your youth will finally start to show.

If you get intuitive guidance to stop and rest, or it tells you that something in your body isn't feeling right, listen to it. Pay attention to what your body is telling you. Give it what it needs. This can be rest, food, or other sustenance that your body yearns for to deal with its lack of available sacral energy.

4. BORROW ENERGY WHEN YOU NEED TO

Without our own Sacral energy, we rely on the borrowed energy of our Generator friends. When we need energy to get something done, it helps to get out among other people so we can absorb and amplify their energy while we complete a task. Absorbing short bursts of energy from other people is both beneficial and useful so we can get things done. We just shouldn't overuse these energy bursts or draw on this energy for long periods. When we do, we not only exhaust ourselves, we also exhaust the person we are drawing energy from.

For example, if you need to finish a university assignment and you're lacking the motivation to complete it, go to a library and finish it off. You can draw on the Sacral energy of other library patrons and complete your work more efficiently than trying it get it all done on your own at home.

The key is to borrow energy for short periods of time only. Remember, Reflectors don't naturally know when enough is enough, so it's important to set yourself time limits for energy borrowing so you don't burn yourself out.

5. ENERGISE IN A POSITIVE CROWD

When you feel depleted, another way to rejuvenate your energy resources is to bask in the positive energy of a crowd. Most Reflectors don't like being around large groups of people. Crowds exhaust us. Busy shopping malls and long queues can completely drain us. I never recommend spending time with crowds in this context.

Some types of crowds, however, can provide an exhilarating and energetically uplifting experience for Reflectors. The energy of a happy, positive crowd can feel amazing and can even be energetically therapeutic.

I still love watching a live local band at a particular bar in my neighbourhood. I go there specifically to dance with some friends for a couple of hours once in a while. Everyone there is usually in a celebratory mood. The music and the sacral energy of people around me enables me to have a great couple of energetic hours while I mill around the dance floor. I always leave with a smile on my face and warmth in my heart.

I also enjoy basking in the energy of a crowd of people watching a sunset. I get an energy buzz from people while they watch the sun go down. I feel an immense sense of contentment. I often get this same feeling when I'm in a beautiful location where everyone is enjoying the scenery or at celebratory occasion such as a New Year's Eve street party.

If you get the chance to be somewhere in a crowd that radiates positivity, joy, and love, you simply must allow yourself the wonderful experience of basking in the elated energy of a crowd. It feels like you're floating on a warm fluffy cloud, uplifting and rejuvenating your spirits.

6. IF YOU'RE UNDER 40, STOP ACTING LIKE A GENERATOR

If you're young enough and still have time on your side, pay particular attention to how you operate your human vehicle. While you may be able to do many things and feel energetically invincible at times, you must give yourself plenty of down time and rest. Use the energy blasts you receive now to set yourself up so you can have a more restful life after 40, when you may not have the same energy reserves.

Tune into your inner guidance system, understand how your openness absorbs and amplifies energy, and listen to your body when it's telling you to slow down. By doing these things, you should be able to avoid total burnout in the future.

Like most things, the more effort you put in now to practice good and healthy habits, the greater the reward will be in the long run.

THE CHALLENGE OF SLEEP

Sleep is an investment in the energy
you need to be effective tomorrow.

\- Tom Rath

EVERYONE NEEDS SLEEP. Without sleep, we don't renew our cells and rest our bodies properly. Sleep is even more vital for the 30% of people with an open Sacral centre, including Reflectors.

Reflectors need more rest and rejuvenation than Generator types. Without a sacral motor, or any of the four motors in the human design chart, sleep is one of the only ways we generate the energy to get through each day. Anything that affects our duration and quality of sleep can significantly impact our lives. Sleep is not only critical for resting our body, but it restores us energetically and is critical to our health. We struggle to function without good sleep.

Sleep is like medicine for Reflectors. Sleep is an important way for us to discharge the energy we pick up from everyone else during the day. It is an essential restorative process that allows us to repair any damage we have done by pushing ourselves too hard energetically using borrowed sacral energy.

Good sleep becomes problematic for Reflectors when we sleep next to Generator types. Often the energy that a Generator continues to emit – that sacral life force energy – can affect our ability to achieve restful sleep. The energy of a Generator can be so big that Reflectors can't relax properly while lying next to them.

What makes it harder for Reflectors is the need to go to bed before being tired. Reflectors often can't fall asleep straight away. We need time to discharge the energies we have picked up from other people during the day. This may cause us to lie awake, overthinking, with our minds still buzzing. We lie there unable to drift off to slumber while our Generator partners are snoring away next to us.

SOLUTION – GET A GOOD NIGHT'S SLEEP

Reflectors need good sleep. To ensure we get enough sleep, we need to go to bed before we are tired. While we're in bed, we should lay down and do something that helps us unwind such as read a book, listen to music, or even watch television. The key is to be laying down for at least 30 minutes before we intend to fall asleep. This helps us to discharge the energy we've picked up during the day and to ease ourselves into slumber.

We should already have a good idea of how many hours of actual sleep we need. Eight hours is a good standard to go by for most people. If eight hours is the amount of actual sleep you need, then you should plan to be in bed for at least eight and a half hours. This allows you to have the time required to discharge other people's energy so you can sleep well for the full eight hours.

As well as sleep duration, sleep quality is equally important. Sleeping properly through the night ensures sufficient restoration. We need to be able to sleep right through the night without disturbance, so we wake up refreshed and revitalized.

Reflectors tend to sleep best alone. When we do, we aren't affected by anyone else's energy while we're in bed. This allows us to have a reasonably undisturbed sleep. Sleeping next to someone can affect our quality of sleep - particularly sleeping next to Generator types. Their sacral motor energy can prevent us from falling asleep and can cause us to have a very disturbed sleep.

Unlike Reflectors, Generators need to go to bed when they are exhausted. If they don't properly exhaust their energy during the day, when they go to bed, they will have a restless sleep. Since we absorb our Generator companion's sacral energy, their restless sleep will typically also affect us. We can sometimes feel or hear their sacral motor energy buzzing during the night. When the Generator is also a snorer or a restless sleeper, this compounds our ability to drift into a restful slumber. It is extremely difficult to sleep with the sensation of an enormous train engine in the bed.

My husband is a Generator and he has a dynamic, intense life force energy. He also has a few sleep issues, so sleeping next to him feels like I've had a wild night out on the town the next day. I wake up looking groggy with puffy eyes and a bad temper. I love snuggling up to him but trying to get a good night's sleep next to him is near impossible.

We now sleep in separate rooms. We spend time in the same bed together when we can and sometimes spend the whole night in the same room. But, most of the time, we sleep separately. This has been so important to the quality of our relationship. I am a much better and healthier person when I have a good night's sleep, and he can relax and sleep however he wants without fear that any slight movement in the night is going to disturb me. It's not conventional, but the more people I talk to about sleeping separately, the more I realise how common it is.

If you can sleep well next to someone, that's great. I encourage it. But, if you can't and you want to be a vibrant, healthy Reflector, it's essential that you do everything you can to get a good night's rest every night. If this means sleeping alone, do it.

If you must sleep next to a Generator, ensure they have exhausted their energy before going to bed. Also, go to bed before them if you can. This way, you can discharge the energy you've absorbed during the day while they're out of the room and hopefully be asleep by the time they come to bed. If you do choose this path, it is beneficial to sleep at least one or two nights alone each week if you can.

Sleeping next to another non-sacral being such as a Manifestor, Projector, or another Reflector can allow you to have a more restful sleep, but not always. It depends on your chart connections.

COACHING TIPS

1. PAY ATTENTION TO HOW YOU FEEL IN THE MORNING

Start paying attention to how you feel when you wake up. If you usually feel well-rested and rejuvenated, you may have no issues with your current sleeping arrangements no matter who you're sleeping next to. If you often wake up tired or you don't feel restored after a good night's sleep, it is important to work out why. Regular disturbed sleep or sleep that doesn't restore you can be the result of not going to bed before you're tired, not getting enough sleep, or sleeping next to someone else.

2. WORK OUT HOW MUCH SLEEP YOU NEED

Work out how much actual sleep you need to feel good in the morning. If you're not sure, plan for eight hours of sleep. Reflectors typically need a lot of sleep, much more than our Generator companions. If you're not sure what length of sleep works best for you, try to use a sleep app or a watch, such as a Fitbit, to track your sleep over time. This can be used to track the length of sleep you need to feel best in the morning. A tracker will also help you establish how much awake time versus actual sleep time you achieve while in bed. This is vital for working out the amount of sleep you need to function optimally.

3. GO TO BED BEFORE YOU'RE TIRED

Once you've worked out how many hours of sleep you need each night, add at least another 30 minutes to this time and spend that amount of time in bed each night. If you have to be awake at 5 a.m., for example, make sure you go to bed at 8:30 p.m. Allow yourself at least 30 minutes to discharge energy so your mind can wind down before you fall asleep. You may notice that you need more sleep. I usually take about an hour to go to sleep, so I allow myself nine hours in bed each night to ensure I get my required eight hours of slumber.

During these 30 minutes, you can do anything as long as you're lying down. Reading and listening to music is good. Scrolling the internet on your phone will suffice, but it doesn't help to completely wind down your thoughts and properly discharge your energy before going to sleep.

4. SLEEP ALONE WHEN YOU CAN

If you share a bed with someone and you wake up tired, look at the Human Design type of your sleeping partner. If they're a Generator type, you may need to sleep in two separate rooms when you can. This doesn't mean you can't ever sleep together. You can at least start the night together or perhaps choose to sleep together a couple of nights each week.

Before you take the drastic measure of separate bedrooms, you may want to try going to bed before them to see if this makes a difference on your ability to get a good night's rest. Also, make sure your Generator sleeping companion is going to bed exhausted and not full of energy. If this works, keep this practice up. If this doesn't make much difference, separate sleeping arrangements are your best option. If you can't sleep like this on a regular basis, try spending at least one or two nights sleeping on your own each week. The extra restorative rest you receive is absolutely worth it.

The Challenge of a Sensitive Immune System

*It is health that is real wealth and
not pieces of gold and silver.*
- Mahatma Gandhi

THE SPLEEN IS THE CENTRE for health. Having an open Spleen means Reflectors have a sensitive immune system. We tend to feel every ailment and get a strong sense of what is going on inside our bodies. This often makes us sensitive to prescription medications and we usually have a lower tolerance to drugs and alcohol.

While sensitivities may not appear early in life, if we haven't taken care of our health and our energy levels during our younger years, we can easily become hyper-sensitive as we reach 35 and beyond.

I ate and drank whatever I wanted up until I was about 35, feeling somewhat invincible. Then, in my late 30s, I began to develop a swarm of health issues. I developed many food intolerances. I could barely drink alcohol anymore without it really affecting me, and I even began to get body and joint pain in areas of my body that had once felt so strong. Exercise, which had always been a part of my life, began to feel like a struggle to complete.

I spent thousands of dollars visiting doctors and natural therapists trying to get to the bottom of my woes. After years of appointments, tests, and many out-of-pocket expenses, I realized that I had just developed a sensitive immune system. Questions swarmed my mind. Was my immune system always sensitive? Had I pushed my health too far believing nothing could affect me? Was it because I acted so long as a Generator type during my younger years that I burned myself out and didn't have the energy to completely recover? I didn't have any answers. The only thing that I knew for sure was that my body was no longer able to function the way it once did.

Now that I'm tuned into my sensitivities, I can sense what is good and bad for me. I can smell and taste how my body will process things. My body has become so sensitive that I can't cope at all on prescription medications. I know my body needs natural remedies and anything that has chemicals, is processed, or is harsh on the body is a no-go zone for me.

I now take vitamin supplements every day which help me to feel vital and healthy. I imagine if I moved out to a remote country town, things could be different. If everything was fresh from paddock to plate, there was minimal pollution in the air, the water was pure, and the air wasn't buzzing with radio waves, I may not need these vitamins to feel good. Since I don't live in such an idyllic world, I'll continue to do whatever is necessary to support my sensitive body so I can continue to play my role as a wise observer of the world.

As we've discussed in a previous chapter, it is not unusual for Reflectors to get sick and burn out as we age. If we haven't stopped pushing ourselves, acting like Generators with sacral life force energy, we are likely to fry our system completely after the age of 40. History has shown that Reflectors can end up with drug and alcohol addictions and serious illnesses if we don't pay attention to our needs. We must move at our own natural pace and minimize stress in our lives.

We have a sensitive immune system, and our complete openness means we absorb and hold onto energy that isn't ours, often burning us out. When we don't slow down and go at our own pace, health issues follow. We may end up with intolerances, long term illnesses, or worse if we don't protect ourselves and take care of our energetic needs.

Solution – Pay Attention to Your Health

Our open Spleen centre gives us a sensitive immune system, which means we suffer more with minor ailments. Our sensitivity here provides us with an early warning signal that lets us know when something isn't right, so we can fix it before it turns into a more serious condition. People with a defined Spleen centre have a strong immune system. When they finally realise they're sick, they are usually very sick because they don't get these early warning signals.

Our open Spleen centre can tell us a lot. All we need to do is pay attention. This is why we should listen to the intuitive messages we receive about our health. Having an early warning signal that lets us know when things aren't quite right internally helps us find ways to resolve these issues before we do even further damage to ourselves. This is why natural medicines are better for our bodies. Our sensitive bodies need gentler therapies.

We have a sampling aura. This means we sample energy from people and the world around us. When the energies we sample aren't healthy, they can impact our own health. When we're in a toxic environment, our health greatly suffers. This is not just physically toxic environments but also mentally and emotionally toxic ones. We need to find ways of protecting ourselves if we must continue to exist in these environments.

There are many different techniques available to protect ourselves from the impact of toxic environments and people. Wrapping ourselves in a bubble of white light before we enter this type of environment is an effective protection technique using visualisation. We can also use smudge sticks or any other techniques that help clear the energy of these places. We need to do all we can to keep our aura clear.

There are some great new therapies that help clear our biofield and remove the energy we collect in our aura. Reflectors tend to have a lot of energy hanging around in our biofield because of our sampling nature. It helps to find a way to totally clear out our biofield first and then continue to keep our aura clean and protected into the future.

If we pay attention to our internal early warning signal and protect ourselves from the toxic energies in our environment, we have a greater chance of living as happy and healthy Reflectors into old age.

Coaching Tips

---

1. STICK WITH NATURAL HOLISTIC MEDICINE

Our sensitive immune system responds better to natural medicines and holistic practices. Prescription drugs can often be too harsh for our systems. There are times we need these, but we should try more natural therapies first if this is an option.

Start to notice how you feel when you're using prescription medications and drugs. Notice if you feel any different when you engage in using more holistic medical approaches. Your body knows what's best for you, so tune in to it.

I find that antibiotics send my stomach completely into a spin. When they kill off the good bacteria in my gut, the bad bacteria return with a vengeance. I also break into cold sores on my mouth when I take penicillin. My personal experience is that my body can't handle the harsh treatments of antibiotics. Sometimes, I have no other choice and I need to take prescription medications. Every time I do, it takes a long time for my body to recover from their side effects. I now only take these harsh medications when absolutely necessary.

When you feel energetically low, get some supporting natural supplements to give yourself a boost. Your body needs all the support it can get to stay healthy and vital.

2. PAY ATTENTION TO YOUR IN-THE-MOMENT INTUITION

When you intuitively sense that something isn't right in your body, pay attention. Your body will tell you what it needs. You may get a message that your liver isn't processing properly. Perhaps you'll feel something not right in your bowel. Pay attention and get it looked at by a doctor if necessary.

Tune in to your body. It will tell you everything you need to know. You may get a sense that you're lacking vitamin C. Purchasing this supplement is a simple solution and it may help you stay healthy if this is what your body needs.

3. PROTECT AND CLEAR YOUR AURA

Regularly clear out your aura using an aura-clearing technique. Anytime you experience a toxic or unhealthy environment or person, clear your aura as soon as you can. Some clearing techniques include:

- Smudging
- Breath work
- Getting out in nature and grounding yourself
- Yin yoga
- Sound therapy – singing bowls, Schumann Resonance, bells, gongs, chimes, etc.
- Essential oils
- Salt baths
- Crystals
- Emotional Freedom Technique
- Reiki
- Bio resonance therapy
- Biofield tuning

When you enter a toxic environment or you notice that your health is being impacted by the people and the environment you are in, the best thing you can do is to leave the environment.

If this is not an option and you must stay within a toxic environment, make sure you protect yourself every day before entering. Then, clear your aura once you've left. Visualising techniques can be an effective way to protect yourself before entering these environments. You can protect your aura by imagining yourself covered in bubble of light or wearing a cloak of protection. Wearing a smoky quartz crystal can also help remove and protect you from negative energy.

Reflectors have a naturally resistant aura. When we know how to use it properly, we can sample energy and then let it slide off of us. This makes it easier to resist succumbing to the unhealthy effects of a toxic environment. Even with our resistant aura, we should still avoid these situations. When you find yourself within these environments, at least have a technique you can draw on that will help protect yourself while you are there.

PART THREE

Connect With People

While Reflectors need a lot of alone time to discharge our energy and to understand who we are, we equally need people to activate us. Without contact with other people, we can't use our ability to tune into our community and become wise about its health and wellbeing.

Other people both activate us and condition us. This means we are often at the mercy of others. How we let them affect us is entirely up to us. We need to understand the impact that other people have on our open centres and what to look out for in other people, so we can live happily and healthily as a Reflector.

This section has three main challenges:

- Energy addiction
- Healthy relationships
- Too much time alone

Each chapter within this section is dedicated to exploring one of these challenges and provides tips for effectively connecting with other people.

THE CHALLENGE OF
ENERGY ADDICTION

Every time you feel yourself being pulled into other people's drama, repeat these words: not my circus, not my monkeys.
- Polish proverb

WITHOUT CONSISTENCY in any of our energy centres, Reflectors are prone to latch on to the energy absorbed from other people's defined energy centres. It's daunting having no consistency. Instead of harnessing our openness, we often try to fill it up in an attempt to feel whole.

With our open Spleen centre, we crave the feel-good energy from people who have a defined Spleen centre. Our open G centre draws us to people who have a defined G centre so we can absorb their strong sense of self and life direction energy. We crave the energy for doing, so we borrow the work force energy of our Generator friends. It feels good to have the energy to get things done. We often find ourselves coming back for more of this borrowed energy, despite the unhealthy effect this has on us when we don't take the time to rest.

It feels great to have willpower energy. We are often drawn to people with a defined Will centre because around them, we feel like we can achieve anything. It feels wonderful to utilize the energy from someone's defined Throat centre and have the temporary ability to turn words into actions. It feels good to feel powerful in this way. Having access to certainty and mental clarity is also very attractive to us. Our mental pressure is temporarily reduced when we spend time with people who have a defined Head and Ajna centre. Like a drug, it feels good to sample these energies. Once we've had a taste, we often come back for more.

The energy from the Solar Plexus centre is where we are most often caught up. This is called the emotional centre. People who have this centre defined often experience an emotional wave of high and low emotions. Through our open Solar Plexus centre, we absorb emotional energy from other people and amplify this back out. Often, we release this emotional energy more intensely than the person who owns it. When they're on an emotional high, we absorb and share their high. Equally, when they're on their emotional low, we experience and often amplify this lower frequency emotional energy. For this reason, Reflectors are sometimes referred to as 'drama addicts.'

Most of the time, amplifying high emotional energy won't get us into too much trouble. Although, it can cause us to seem intense or dramatic. Amplifying low emotional energy can have a much greater impact on both ourselves and other people. For example, anger is an emotion that can get out of control if we let it take over.

When I lived with someone who had clear anger issues and often had angry periods during his emotional wave, I found myself at times becoming overwhelmed with angry thoughts and actions. Once, my amplification of his energy was so intense, I felt an overwhelming desire to punch him. I'd never felt like that before and I haven't felt like this since. His anger overwhelmed me. I got called all sorts of names during that relationship due to my amplification of his emotional energy.

Holding on to low emotional energy can be really overwhelming for Reflectors. It can consume us. When we feel a pang of anger or sadness, our bodies instantly want to express it back out physically or vocally. As children, if we live in an emotionally unhealthy environment, we are often perceived as a problem child because we absorb and amplify all of the family's emotional energy. We can even be blamed as the cause of the family problems. This absorbed emotional energy comes out of us in many different ways when we're growing up.

When I was a very young girl and my parents were having relationship issues, my eyesight diminished, and I temporarily needed to wear glasses. Relatives also recall me being destructive around this same timeframe, literally throwing things out of cupboards and boxes, acting out and making a mess.

When we feel intense emotional energy, we need to look at what is happening around us and who we are amplifying. This energy usually isn't ours. When we're completely away from other people, we generally feel emotionally stable. We simply don't experience a wave of emotions like people with a defined Solar Plexus centre.

When we spend a lot of time with someone who is emotionally defined and get a taste of their emotional high and low energy, like a drug, it can feel great to be riding on the fumes of someone's emotional high. We can crave these emotional highs because they allow us to feel great, and without a defined Spleen centre, we don't naturally have feel-good energy.

When we're in an unhealthy situation and these emotional highs are no longer available to us, we can settle for feeling someone's low emotional energy. We may even push people into an emotionally low state, so we can sniff on the fumes of their lower emotions just to receive our own emotional 'hit.' Feeling something can seem better than feeling nothing at all. Just like any addiction, we can be so consumed with our desire to feel something emotionally, that we'll trigger any emotional response from someone just so we can absorb and amplify their energy.

When I was in a dysfunctional relationship and it wasn't going well, I recall sometimes pushing my partner when he was on an emotional low. This was to spark him into an argument so I could feel something. When we argued, I was more emotionally charged than I've ever been in my life. While this didn't feel good, it felt better than feeling complete emptiness, which is what I felt most of the time when I was with him. We no longer shared the emotional highs that I had grown to adore with him, and instead, the relationship was like an emotional vacuum. Rather than do what I should have done and leave the relationship, I stayed around pushing to experience those emotional lows as much as possible, so I felt at least something after all the years of being together.

It's easy for Reflectors to identify with other people's energy as though it's our own. Our openness makes us sensitive to everyone and everything around us. It can be difficult to distinguish between what does and doesn't belong to us. If we don't learn to release this energy, it can be both frustrating and unhealthy for us in the long term. When we don't understand how our openness affects us, we can easily become an addict of other people's energy. We can crave an energetic hit from their defined energy centres because their strong consistent energy fills us up, and it temporarily feels good.

SOLUTION – REMOVE AND PROTECT YOURSELF FROM OTHER PEOPLE'S ENERGY

Notice when you feel caught up in the energy of other people. Notice when this is becoming like an addiction that you struggle to control. If you sense yourself relying on the energy of other people around you and you struggle to step away from it, it may be time to acknowledge that you have an energy addiction.

The best thing you can do in that moment is to remove yourself from the person with the energy that you've become addicted to. You may need to get away from that person for a few weeks if the addiction is really bad. Give yourself a whole month away from them ideally on your own if you can. This will allow you to really detangle yourself from their energy and their conditioning. This is why travel is so beneficial. Removing yourself from familiar environments and people allows you to be more present without your usual energetic influences.

While you need to protect yourself from the addictive nature of all energy centre energies, dealing with emotional energy needs more regular management. Our open Solar Plexus centre makes us emotionally empathetic because we feel the emotional energy of other people. To properly equip yourself to manage this energy, you need to pay attention to how you feel emotionally at any given time. When you feel a rush of emotional energy come through you, notice what is going on around you. Sometimes, this emotional energy comes from the greater world around you or from the planetary transits which also impact you. Most of the time, this emotional energy is absorbed from the people around you.

Once you sense emotional energy stirring within, choose how you will manage it. You can feel these emotions and then let them pass through you, or you can hold onto them, amplify them, and express them externally. When you sense a feeling of happiness come through you, observe where it's come from and then allow yourself to enjoy the emotion. When you notice a lower emotion take hold, observe where it's from and feel it, but then release it so you don't amplify it in an unhealthy way.

When someone is on their emotional low and you begin to feel their emotional energy, do what you can to remove yourself from them. Even 15 minutes away from them can be enough to discharge their absorbed emotional energy so it doesn't take hold of you and become amplified.

If you find yourself in an argument with someone, tune into your experience of these emotions and how they have a hold of you. Simply noticing emotional energy can be enough for it to subside. Remove yourself completely from this person if you can. This is a more effective technique because the emotional energy is discharged entirely once you're away from their influence.

I had intense arguments with my mother as a girl. We both have an open Solar Plexus centre, so when we sense low emotional energy around us, we are both affected. She'd tell me off, and I would yell back at her more intensely with my open Throat centre energy pushing to be heard over her defined Throat centre energy. This would cause her to raise her voice and then I'd get louder and so on. It would be like a fireball of emotion during those blasts of emotional energy.

What was always astonishing to those around us was that, 30 minutes later, we would both be back to normal chatting, hugging, and getting on with whatever we were doing as though nothing had happened. Neither of us could hold this emotional energy for long, and as soon as it had discharged, it was gone. Years later, I couldn't understand why my friends and boyfriends took so long to get over heated arguments. I would be completely over it within a few minutes and they were still harbouring and stewing on their emotions for what seemed like way too long. They clearly needed to wait through their emotional wave, which I didn't understand at the time. Had I known this, it would have saved me years of emotional heartache.

Take note of the people in your life who have a defined Solar Plexus centre. When you notice they're on an emotional low, put strategies in place to prevent yourself from being swept up in their emotional energy. You may choose to stay away from them during these times or find other ways to support yourself, so you don't become overtaken by their energy. You may choose to spend more time in meditation during these periods or out in nature. You need to find ways to lift yourself up, so you don't become entangled in their emotions. This is also an important time to be a screen rather than a sponge, filtering their emotional energy rather than absorbing it.

When I sense low emotional energy begin to penetrate me, I do what I can to take myself away from that person straight away. Sometimes, I let them know that I just need to step away for a moment because I'm feeling emotionally overwhelmed and it's nothing personal. This way, it doesn't sound like I'm blaming them for the emotional energy that's brewing. Instead, I'm proactively ensuring that I don't become emotionally entwined with them.

By making better choices while around these emotional energies, you can enjoy the emotional highs and prevent yourself from amplifying intense low emotional energy. Protecting yourself from emotional energy is something you will constantly need to deal with unless you're living as a hermit. Getting caught up in and addicted to energy from other people's defined centres is something you can control by spending more time alone and by getting to know yourself better.

COACHING TIPS

1. DETERMINE IF YOU'RE AN ENERGY ADDICT

Determine if you're addicted to the energy of other people. Notice if you rely on energy from other people's defined energy centres and consider your relationship with that energy. Ask yourself:

- Do you rely on other people to feel good?
- Do you always draw on other people's energy to get things done?
- Are you holding on too tightly to someone else's identity and direction and assuming these yourself?
- Do you rely on other people for mental clarity and certainty?
- Do you feel the need to be around other people all the time?
- Do you coax an emotional response from someone so you can feel their emotions?
- Do you rarely spend time alone?

If you answered yes to any of these questions, chances are you're an energy addict.

2. REMOVE YOURSELF FROM THE ENERGY SOURCE

The best way to recover from an energy addiction is to remove yourself entirely from the source of the addiction. It can be hard to let go of this energy while in the presence of the energy source you're absorbing. If you remove yourself completely from this person and their energy, you'll have an easier time releasing the energy and healing yourself from your addiction to it.

Don't swap this person's energy for someone else's energy once you've removed yourself from them. You have a much better chance of finding your authentic self when you're alone and without other people's influencing energies. Your own gifts and potential are more fully realized. When you truly find yourself, you'll no longer crave the energy of other people.

When you finally have the time and space you need to fully engage with yourself and your openness, you will no longer need other people's energy to fill you up because you won't feel a void in these open centres. You can then properly utilize your Teflon aura to sample energy without developing an attachment to it.

3. DEAL WITH EMOTIONAL ENERGY

a) Ask "is this my emotion?"

When you're feeling emotional, always ask yourself "is this my emotion?" By understanding what and who is influencing the emotions you experience, you can begin to unravel yourself from the emotions of other people and not become a drama addict.

Notice who's around when you feel emotional. Emotional energy can come from anybody in the vicinity, even when you're not directly interacting with them. For example, in a workplace or a public space, you can pick up on the emotional energy of anybody nearby.

b) Remove yourself from the emotional trigger

When you've become emotionally triggered or caught up in someone else's emotions, remove yourself from this person for at least 15 minutes to discharge their emotional influence. In a heated argument, for example, remove yourself and leave the resolution to a time when the emotional energy has dissipated.

When you notice someone is on an emotional low, it may be best to avoid them when you can. This saves you from becoming caught up in their emotional energy. If this is someone you live with, find ways to give them space and to keep them from impacting you.

Spend as much time alone as you can. This will help you disengage from their emotional energy. Anything you do to protect yourself from emotional energy helps.

4. STOP BEING AN ENERGY ADDICT

Ask yourself if you are someone who craves and seeks other people to feel good and whole. Consider if you actively seek people's energy in an attempt to feel something.

If you've become an energy addict, it's time to get out of this unhealthy cycle. Deal with any suppressed feelings you have as a result of your life conditioning and protect yourself by being a screen and not a sponge of other people's influencing energy. Only you can change how you manage another person's energy. At the very least, pack your bags and get away on your own for a while. You'll be surprised how effective this method is in removing your energy addiction.

THE CHALLENGE OF HEALTHY RELATIONSHIPS

You are not required to set yourself on
fire to keep other people warm.

- Unknown

RELATIONSHIPS FEEL good for Reflectors. We like the consistent energy of a partner in our lives to balance our own inconsistencies. They feel like a port in our storm of energetic inconsistency. We fill our open centres by absorbing their consistent energies, and this helps us to feel good while they're around. We may even begin to rely on their energetic stability to centre and calm us. We like the predictability of knowing our partner's aura. Physical touch is also often important to us, because it can help ground us. Being in a relationship caters to our need for touch and affection.

Choosing the right partner and having healthy relationships is a huge challenge for Reflectors. Several aspects of our design can work against us when it comes to finding a partner who is right for us. One of the biggest problems with relationships for Reflectors is that we can become clingy and codependent because of our openness. These difficulties arise mainly due to our potential for conditioning and our open Spleen and open G centres.

We become attached to people who have a defined Spleen centre because they have 'feel good' energy, something we don't innately have. Thanks to our open G centre, Reflectors sense the beauty in everyone. When we are living our design, we don't see people for their life conditioning and their resulting actions, but rather we feel the truth of who they really are. We see beyond their flaws and external imperfect expressions and easily fall in love with someone's potential. This means we can potentially fall in love with anyone.

Not only does our open G centre allow us to see the beauty in everyone, it also causes us to absorb and take on the identity and life direction of our partner. The longer we spend with someone, the greater our chance of merging with them. We can easily get caught up living someone else's life due to our open G centre. It can be difficult to distinguish between our partner and ourselves after we've lived with them for a while. We can become co-dependent with them. Their life path becomes ours. Our life direction and identity become intertwined with theirs.

An ex-partner wrote me a letter after he'd left me. In the letter, he said that I'd faked liking the things he liked during our relationship. He said that, before I met him, I wasn't into indie music and I had somehow stolen his identity in demonstrating my enjoyment of it while in the relationship. While I never understood this at the time, he was correct in a way. I had been amplifying his very defined G centre. My open G centre allowed me to experience his feelings of self and caused me to truly enjoy some of the things he enjoyed. Of course, once our relationship ended, I stopped listening to this type of music, because it was his passion for this music that I had picked up on and enjoyed while I was with him.

Losing a partner is often overwhelming. For us, it feels like we are literally losing a part of ourselves and our identity.

Once we latch onto someone's identify and direction, we have a hard time letting go because our open Spleen centre causes us to hold onto things longer than we should – even when the relationship is no longer beneficial. We often stay in relationships with the wrong people because we see the truth of someone beneath their conditioning. We may even attempt to rescue them from their own conditioning and hope they will love us forever if we save them from themselves. This can cause us to justify staying in an unhealthy, even abusive, relationship.

When a partner treats us badly, we may justify their behavior because we know it isn't actually about us but rather due to their past conditioning. We can easily forgive partners for this reason and allow them to treat us in ways that are less than we deserve.

I recall saying to a friend at one point in my life, "He tried to choke me, but it's okay. I'm angry at him, but he didn't really mean it or want to hurt me. He is just frustrated at his own inability to articulate how he feels due to his troubled childhood." This wasn't forgiving his behaviour. I merely understood why he acted this way and I didn't take it personally.

Like the 'better the devil we know' adage, we hold on to what is familiar and consistent, holding onto someone's potential, even when we know it's not good for us. Staying in these relationships isn't healthy for us and our own needs typically go unmet. Reflectors mirror whoever we're with. If we're with an unhealthy and unstable person, we will further exasperate our partner's issues because we mirror them back. The effects of staying in an unhealthy relationship are detrimental to a Reflector's health and well-being.

I was once in a relationship with a man who had very little love and appreciation for himself. As a Reflector, I could see underneath his conditioning the true and beautiful essence that he was. I did everything I could to help him see his own gorgeous potential while we were together. Even though I could see this beauty and I loved him unconditionally, he was unable to see this in himself.

After a few years of living together, I began to lose the love and appreciation I had for myself. Instead of picking him up and drawing him into the higher vibration of love and acceptance that I had for him, I became conditioned to think and feel about myself the way he did about himself. For the few extra years that I lived with him, I developed low self-esteem and no longer accepted or approved of myself. He eventually ended the relationship, expressing to me his clear disdain at the person I'd become, which I realise now was the embodiment and reflection of himself. His words of disgust for me were really about himself. In the end, he saw me as his enemy. Instead of dealing with his own demons, he demonized me.

It took me a couple of years to break free of the conditioning from this relationship. Five years with someone changed me so much that I no longer recognised myself. Unravelling my beliefs, thoughts, and feelings that I'd become conditioned to believe were my own, from what was really me, was a difficult process, but it was entirely liberating once I got through to the other side. I finally fell in love with myself because I began to see myself naked, free from my conditioning, for the very first time.

SOLUTION – CHOOSE YOUR PARTNER WISELY

Reflectors crave consistency. We yearn for stability externally because we have so much inconsistency within ourselves. Relationships can be a great way to have consistency in our lives. But, we should only engage in relationships that are healthy for us. Otherwise, we are at the mercy of being conditioned by our partners and this damages us immensely if we let it.

When we are in a healthy relationship, we thrive. The support we get from someone who loves us and is reliable allows us to have a steady platform from which we can launch ourselves into the world. From this stable platform, we can truly get out there and experience the world as a Reflector knowing that we have a beacon of light that we can return to and a platform to rest upon when weathering a storm.

Being in an unhealthy relationship can be detrimental to our own health and well-being. A bad relationship can cause our open centres complete havoc. When a relationship doesn't give us the stable platform we need, we spend all our time trying to prove our worth to our partner. We also hang on to them so tightly they often feel like we're drowning them.

The key for us in relationships is consistency. Even within an open relationship, we can get consistency from a partner. If our partner reassures us of what is and what isn't in the relationship and they provide a stable foundation for us to base our relationship on, this gives us all the stability we need.

The Challenge of Healthy Relationships

I've always been a strong, independent person. I like space and alone time like most Reflectors. In one of my relationships, my partner, who was a Manifesting Generator with an identity crisis, was unable to give me any stability. Even though we lived together and travelled around the world together, it always felt like he had one foot out the door. I sensed he would leave me high and dry at any moment.

Because I was in love with him and I grew accustomed to having his energy in my life, I clung on to the memories of happy times in the early stages of our relationship. But, he would literally run away when things got tough or we had an argument. And, silly old clingy Reflector me would literally chase after him.

My open Spleen attachment to him caused me to beg him to stay with me every time he threatened to leave. I was constantly on edge, holding on for dear life. He told me I wanted more commitment than he did, which I didn't understand because I really wasn't looking at settling down or anything at that stage. I just wanted to travel the world with him and enjoy life. Because he was a Manifesting Generator who wanted the freedom to do things at his own speed and would forget to inform me about things he was doing, my clinginess made him feel trapped. I felt completely left behind because he went ahead and did things all the time without letting me know.

Needless to say, it wasn't a healthy relationship, and the longer I stayed with him, the worse it became. His inability to be a stable platform for me and his own feelings of inadequacy left me feeling terribly wounded. I totally lost myself in that relationship. I only wish at that time in my life I'd known about Human Design to make sense of it sooner.

When we are in a healthy relationship with someone who can give us the consistent and reliable energy that we need, we can truly bloom as Reflectors.

When I finally met my husband, for the first time I understood what it meant to truly become the fullest, happiest, and best version of myself. He is my rock. I know he will be there for me no matter what, and this gives me the freedom to be myself. I am far from clingy with him. If anything, I am more independent than ever and have more drive to pursue my own things. He allows me to be me, which enables me to be a supportive partner to him without the clinginess and neediness of my past relationships.

It is very easy for Reflectors to fall for people because we have this ability to see into the heart of who they are. Knowing we have this incredible ability, it's important that we don't let this cloud our judgement about who we fall in love with.

Be wise in your choices when allowing someone into your aura, and particularly into your heart. Ask yourself how they make you feel. Then, determine if they can give you the stability that you need from a partner. Be honest with yourself. After all, these choices will affect you considerably. Stay strong when you need to. Sure, it's important to pay attention to how you feel about them, but also look at what they do and say and what type of life they've had so far. We can almost fall in love with anybody...so choose wisely.

Many of my ex-partners came back to me years later to say they were sorry for the way things turned out. Some of them even wanted to start something up again. This happens with many Reflectors. If you know that they are bad for you in the long run, don't let yourself get sucked into their aura again and therefore their life.

If you have a partner or live with someone and it feels right to continue to do so, understand how you impact each other. There will be some things you feel really connected about and other things you will probably have to compromise on.

Within our unique Human Design blueprint, we each have gates that give us our unique characteristics. Even as Reflectors, we have defined gates that make us unique and different from each other. Within our body chart, there are channels (which look like lines) that connect the Human Design energy centres to one another. Each channel has a gate at either end. When someone has both gates of a channel defined in their Human Design chart, it means they have this channel defined. This also makes the two centres either side of the channel defined in their chart. This is how their Human Design type is determined. Reflectors don't have any channels, and therefore we don't have any of the centres defined. All we have is gates.

When we spend time with another person, we connect with them through these gates and channels. When we meet someone who has a gate on the opposite side of the channel to one of our gates (we have one gate of the channel and they have the other gate), we have what is called an attraction connection. This means we are attracted energetically to the other person. This isn't necessarily sexual attraction (although this can be one of the effects). It's more like yin and yang coming together in perfect harmony over a particular interest/trait. It feels great to connect with people who have these opposing gates because we light each other up, so to speak.

When we spend time with someone who has both gates in a channel and we have only one of these gates, this is called a compromise channel. The person who has only one gate has to compromise on that particular trait to the person who has the whole channel.

Reflectors don't have any channels in our chart. Therefore, when we form a channel of compromise with someone, we are always the one who has to compromise. It helps to be aware of this and find a way to live with these compromises if we choose to spend a lot of time with someone.

My husband and I both have the gate of impact. We both have a desire to be seen and to make an impact. He has the whole channel, meaning he also has the opposing gate. Therefore, when we're both in a situation where we want to be seen and heard, he typically wins. He has more energetic power here because he has the full channel. To prevent arguments, I often have to back down and, in this instance, allow him to have the most impact. I have to compromise on my need to be seen and make an impact because this is one of our compromise connections.

When we understand why we need to compromise in areas of our lives, we can take the power struggle out of it and see it as it truly is: the way we're designed. This knowledge helps prevent this affecting how we experience ourselves and our relationships. At the beginning of a new relationship or friendship, it can be handy to learn about these channels of compromise early on so we can understand them and decide if they are something we can live with or not.

It does sometimes feel unfair that we are always the ones who need to compromise. But, armed with this knowledge, we can find ways to work with these compromises within our relationships.

COACHING TIPS

1. LEAVE A RELATIONSHIP THAT IS
NO LONGER HEALTHY FOR YOU

This is obviously easier said than done. If you find yourself in a relationship that doesn't feel good or right, it may be time to end it. If you feel clingy or nervous and apprehensive about your partner, they may not be the right person for you. You need to be in a relationship that provides you stability and consistency. If you're not getting this – it's time to move on.

2. CHOOSE A PARTNER WHO GIVES
YOU STABILITY AND CONSISTENCY

When looking for a new partner, be sure to notice how you feel around them. And, I'm not referring to all that sexual chemistry you may be feeling. Chemistry serves a purpose, but it's not the key ingredient in the type of relationship that is best for a Reflector.

What you need to look for is whether this person gives you a sense of stability or security. Do they help you feel safe with your feelings? Do you feel like they will be there for you through good and bad times? Are they making an effort to show you that they want you in their life?

Reflectors do well with a lot of love. It also helps to have a partner who likes physical affection. Reflectors often need a lot of snuggling and cuddling, so it is an added bonus if they offer you this. Choose a partner who isn't afraid to show you this love. Love and consistency build the steady platform you need in your life.

You don't have to be in a traditional relationship to receive love and stability from a partner. You can be in an open relationship where you both share intimacy with other people and still have a partner who gives you the stability and consistency you need.

It helps to be with someone who has high self-esteem, is a happy person, and who has a strong sense of who they are. As a Reflector, you amplify their energy, thoughts, feelings, and emotions more than you reflect anyone else, so it is highly beneficial to reflect someone who is of healthy mind and spirit. If not, this can bring you down.

3. KNOW THE DIFFERENCE BETWEEN YOU AND YOUR PARTNER

Reflectors benefit from knowing themselves before entering into relationships. When you know what is you and what is not you, you can more easily identify when you are picking up energy, thoughts, and emotions that don't belong to you.

It's easy to get caught up in your partner's thoughts, feelings, and emotions and lose track of your own. Therefore, it's important to spend time alone as often as you can away from your partner's aura to discharge their energy and notice your own. Notice how you feel in your partner's presence and then, when you've spent time completely away from them for at least 15 minutes, notice if you still feel this way. If not, then you can rely on that feeling or thought actually belonging to your partner. Spending time alone helps you to really get in touch with who you are so you can identify when you're picking up the energy of your partner.

By paying attention and finding ways to discharge the energy you've picked up from your partner, you can more easily identify what is naturally you and what aspects of you have been absorbed from your partner and then amplified. This prevents your partner's energy from consuming you, and you can stay aligned to your own identity without getting lost in theirs.

THE CHALLENGE OF TOO MUCH ALONE TIME

*Man is, at one and the same time, a
solitary being and a social being.*
\- Albert Einstein

We KNOW THAT REFLECTORS need as much rest as possible. We need plenty of sleep, and it's important that we don't push and overwork ourselves. We also need lots of time alone to discharge the energy of other people and replenish ourselves. We also need plenty of alone time so that we don't become addicted to the consistent energy of other people. While alone time is essential to life as a healthy Reflector, it is vital that we don't spend too much time alone.

Too much time alone can cause us to feel even less energetic and motivated. We need other people to activate us so we can draw on their energy from time to time to keep us moving in the right direction. Too much time alone can leave us completely unmotivated and sometimes without the energy to get back out into the world.

When we are tucked away from other people, we can easily lose touch with reality and become reclusive. While we may survive for a long time like this, it doesn't allow us to fulfil our role. We are here for other people. We need to sample them so we can be wise observers and guide humanity forward.

SOLUTION – BALANCE YOUR TIME SPENT ALONE AND WITH OTHERS

Once we've spent enough time alone getting to know our authentic selves beneath our energetic conditioning, we need to find a balance between alone time and time with other people. Reflectors need people to activate us. We are designed to sample the world around us, including other people, so we can become wise about thoughts, feelings, communication, love, time, intuition, health, energy, value, and emotions. We can't become wise by spending most of our lives alone. We need to visit the community from time to time so we can become wise observers of it.

Reflectors need to find a balance between being alone and spending time among other people. When we don't spend time with other people, we can spiral into a chasm of melancholy and avoid life. Without the vital energy that we pick up from other people, it can feel impossible to find the motivation to function as a normal human being.

I love my time alone. I need it to discharge the energy of others and bask in just being in the moment. I can do this for days at a time, but eventually, if I stay this way for too long, things begin to change within me. I start to dread going out in public. I become insular and even avoid answering the phone because I don't want to deal with anyone. The fewer connections I have, the more disconnected I become.

The longer I stay alone – locked away from others, the worse this feeling gets. I often have to literally drag myself out of the house to be around other people. However, once I'm in the company of other people again, it feels great. I realise what I've been missing.

As long as the people I mix with are generally positive, I get a buzz of energy from them. Often, I feel motivated straight away to do something that hasn't stirred in me for a while. Other times, I just feel happy and content while in their presence.

Staying at home in your sanctuary for too long is not healthy for Reflectors. Your sanctuary should be a place where you visit to discharge the energy of others and spend time in the moment with yourself. That is all. It is not a cave that you should disappear to, never to be seen again. This is a recipe for disaster and can be the very reason why Reflectors get so overwhelmed by life. Once you've spent time alone for long enough to find yourself, you should come out into the world and be a part of it again.

When you get caught up alone for too long and you lose your desire to interact with others, push through this and get back out there. Come out to play in the world from time to time. You won't regret it. Just make sure the people you come out to play with are people who are healthy for you to be around. Alone time, away from other people, is essential. But, too much alone time isn't healthy for a Reflector and it's not what we're designed for.

Coaching Tips

1. GET OUT OF THE HOUSE

If you work alone, ensure you find several occasions during the week to connect with other people. This could be socially, through work opportunities, or at the very least, take yourself out to a busy café and work from there.

I often meet a friend at a café in the morning for breakfast and then go home to work alone. This gives me the energy I need to power through the day. I am often more productive during these days and feel a greater sense of achievement from my day (even if I don't end up doing a lot of work).

2. PAY ATTENTION TO HOW YOU FEEL

If you're spending a lot of time alone and you feel content and productive, this is great. Keep doing what you're doing. When you start to notice this change, it's time to reconnect with other people. The longer you leave it, the harder this becomes.

You may mentally know that you need to get out there and feel the good vibes of other people, but you may physically find this a challenge. You may struggle to find the motivation to take action. This is when you need to push yourself to get out and connect with other people.

Sometimes it helps to set regular appointments and catch-ups with other people that force you to get out of the house. This ensures you don't spend too much time alone and then struggle to get out again. Explain to a friend or two about your need to be social every now and then. This is a great way to enable a lifeline of friends who drag you out of hibernation when required.

3. CONNECT WITH PEOPLE WHO FEEL GOOD

Since we absorb and reflect back the energy of other people, it is important that we spend time around people that help us to feel good. Hanging out with stressed friends and family or people who are negative won't necessarily help you to feel better and give you the energy hike you need. When you are at risk of spending too much time alone, you need to ensure the people you do end up spending time with to break your cycle of solitude, give you the positive lift that you need. You risk being pushed deeper into your desire for alone time when your only experiences with other people are negative ones.

PART FOUR

Find Sustainable Work

REFLECTORS ARE NOT DESIGNED to be builders of the world like Generator types. We simply haven't got the same workforce energy to sustain working in the expected traditional way. This means we need to be deliberate and intentional in the type of work we chose to engage in, so we are still capable of earning a wage to meet our needs.

This section has two main challenges:

- Traditional work
- Working after 40

Each chapter within this section is dedicated to exploring one of these challenges and provides tips for effectively working as a Reflector.

THE CHALLENGE OF TRADITIONAL WORK

Go where the weather suits your clothes.
- Harry Nilsson

WORK IS A UNIQUE CHALLENGE for Reflectors. Without sustainable energy, Reflectors struggle to work in a traditional 9 to 5 job and a typical 40-hour working week. We simply don't have the energy for it. Sure, we can fake it for a while by drawing on the sacral energy of other people, but this isn't viable for the long term.

Not only do Reflectors struggle with five days of continuous eight-hour work, we also have a desire for variety and variability in our day. The mere mundaneness of a traditional job can really suck the life out of us.

Being on time is also a challenge due to our open Spleen centre. In a world where it is not only frowned upon to be late, but there's an expectation for people to get to work early, Reflectors can become stressed and overwhelmed trying to meet these requirements. It also feels bad when other people judge us as unreliable because we struggle to meet these time obligations.

The first month or so in a new job can be a difficult for Reflectors. When we do find a job working with other people, it can take us a month to find our place in the team and to feel out our role. We need a lunar cycle, at least, to establish where we fit within a new work environment and within the team dynamic. During this time, others may judge us and not yet understand us, making it difficult for us to establish connections at first. Once we settle into a new workplace and a new role, other people typically gravitate toward us. We can then finally establish solid working relationships.

The final challenge for Reflectors in the workplace is caused by our openness. We absorb the energy, emotions, feelings, and thoughts of the people we work with through our nine open centres. Being around people and these energies eight hours a day can be quite overwhelming. When we work in happy, enjoyable, and positive work environments, we reflect this by feeling good and inspired in the workplace. When we work in toxic work environments, we often become sick, stressed, and generally unable to function properly.

In my last traditional job, I worked in a huge corporate environment that was known for having a terrible work culture. The large project I was engaged to work on was problematic. The person managing the project was disliked by many and considered untrustworthy. They had a long list of project issues and incompetent managers who were causing a lot of staff to feel insecure in the work environment.

After a month at that job, I noticed my health starting to deteriorate. I stopped sleeping well. I had what felt like a continuous cold. I even started to get a nervous twitch. While I was externally managing my role and doing a reasonably good job of managing others, I was internally crumbling.

The Challenge of Traditional Work

During my brief three months in that job, I was bought to tears twice while at work. Prior to that, the last time I cried on a job was at 18 years old working as a door-to-door salesperson. But now, I was a grown woman, and this was a senior role with a huge responsibility to deliver an important project. And, here I was crying in my office. In that moment, I realised just how toxic the environment was. Like a canary in a coalmine, my breakdown was the early warning signal that all was not well in that workplace and environment.

Once I realised this, I resigned from that job straight away. It took me a few months to recover from my time in that toxic environment. As it turned out, I left just before things got even worse.

Engaging in traditional work is a major challenge for Reflectors. We don't have the energy to sustain the expected 9 to 5, 40-hour working week. We struggle with mundane repetitive tasks. Sticking to a defined schedule with deadlines and time constraints is really difficult for us. We absorb, and are impacted by, people energy and the culture within a work environment; we much prefer to go with the flow of our energy in the moment. It takes us a month or more to find our place within a team. To top it off, other people don't understand this and make all sorts of judgements about us for not being able to conform within the traditional work mould. Reflectors are simply not designed for traditional work.

Solution – Find a Sustainable Way to Work

Reflectors should engage in work that is less traditional. This means you should look for jobs that have more flexibility in working hours or at least don't require such long work periods. Establish how much work you can healthily achieve each week and the type of work that you can continue to do without burning out. Then, look for work that fits these requirements.

Not having the energy to work in a traditional job shouldn't be an excuse to stay at home on the couch and refuse to do anything. Especially when we are young. Reflectors have the ability to work and be good at it. We just need to find a way to use our energy and resources wisely so we can sustain ourselves.

If you must work in a traditional job, there are a few things you can do to make it a healthier and more enjoyable experience. The key is to choose these traditional jobs wisely. For a start, search for work that offers flexibility in working hours or at least start times.

I've found that my natural start time is 10 a.m. It takes me time in the morning to wake and complete a few daily routines that help keep me healthy. When I make appointments or meetings that start at 10 a.m., I am more likely to be on time and without stress. I'm a night owl, so if that means I work later in the day or the evening, that's fine with me.

Learn what you can about the team and the organisational culture before accepting a job. If you discover the culture within the workplace is toxic or the team has a reputation for being hard to work with, it may be best to find another job.

Choose a work environment that feels good, especially if you spend a lot of time there. If you can, visit the workplace before accepting a job to get a sense of how it feels. Remember, finding your right place is very important as a Reflector. Do what you can to ensure your workplace feels good to you.

It takes about a month to find your place in a team and to feel right in your role. If possible, establish an exit strategy before accepting a job. If you decide the job is not right for you after the first month or two, you have an exit plan in place to make a smooth transition out. Some workplaces offer new starters a three-month probationary period. This not only gives the employer a cooling off period, but it also gives you time to determine if the role, your team, the culture, and the work environment are right for you.

Reflectors have an important role to play in the world. Working traditionally is not what we are designed for. When we try to work like our Generator colleagues, things don't always flow smoothly for us. We are here to be wise and to serve other people. When we look after our health and follow our lunar cycle decision-making strategy, we have the potential for gaining great wisdom. Burned out, struggling Reflectors are unable to play their assigned role.

We are here to sample. We become more capable of fulfilling our design when we try different types of work. Our openness means we learn a lot about people and the world around us and we adapt to most situations and any type of job. We can also successfully change careers many times during our lives, which helps us ensure that life doesn't get too mundane. We benefit from embracing this about ourselves. Open yourself to the endless possibilities of work opportunities that aren't necessarily traditional.

If you currently work somewhere that doesn't feel good or your health is at risk, it may be time to start looking for a new job. Use your wisdom to understand what type of work interests you and work towards finding a job that fulfils your needs as a Reflector, both energetically and spiritually.

COACHING TIPS

1. CHOOSE WORK THAT ISN'T 9 TO 5

Find work that suits your energetic needs. If you're a night owl, find work that you can do in the evening. If you feel better working at your own pace, find a job that gives you this flexibility. Determine your most effective way of working if you must work to earn an income. Find work that gives you more control and flexibility over when and how you work. If you can afford to work part-time, give yourself the benefit of not having to commit to a standard 40-hour working week. Do whatever you can to secure work that allows you to operate optimally as a Reflector.

2. IF YOU MUST WORK TRADITIONALLY, FIND A FLEXIBLE WORKPLACE

Finding work that isn't 9 to 5 may not be an option. If this is the case, find an employer or a career that offers flexibility. Flexibility means you have options about when you work, or at least your start times. It means you have flexibility in how you work or where you work, including work-from-home options. Look for employers or work options that give you the opportunity to tailor how you work your 40-hour week. Also, select work environments that feel good to be in. This will make a huge difference in your overall work experience.

3. BEFORE YOU ACCEPT A JOB, UNDERSTAND THE ORGANISATIONAL CULTURE

Do your research into an organisation or business before you start a new job. Talk to people who work there. Look for online reviews. Ask the hiring manager questions. Do whatever you can to gather insight about the team, the organisation, and how they function. If red flags are raised during your investigation, suggesting the organisational culture is toxic and the team don't work well together, this may be enough evidence to look elsewhere. Remember, as a Reflector you will reflect the health of the team and the environment. If they aren't functioning well, your health will ultimately suffer if you end up working there.

4. HAVE AN EXIT STRATEGY

When you start a new job, have an exit strategy or backup plan in case it doesn't work out. It takes Reflectors a month or more to find our place in a team and feel out a new role. This is a long time to wait and see if a job is right for you. When you start a new job, it helps to have an exit strategy in place.

Ask for a probationary period when commecing a new role. This gives you and the employer a 'get out' clause, allowing you to part ways if it doesn't work out. This makes it easier for you to resign if the job doesn't feel right for you within the first couple of months, no questions asked.

Have a backup plan in place that you can implement if the job doesn't work out. Ensure you can make an easy transition out of the job if necessary. Unless money isn't an issue, you'll need a way to financially support yourself during the transition period. You can set yourself up with another income stream during your transition period or another job to go straight into.

Alternatively, set money aside to cover this period. During the first couple of months in a new job, save some money as part of your backup plan. If you leave the job early, you can fund yourself with this money during your transition period while you look for other work.

As part of your backup plan, you may choose to continue to look for other jobs during this initial work period. Have your resume ready to go if you sense the job may not work out. You may even find casual intermittent work that you can easily turn to if you need to pull the pin on your new job.

After a month or so, you should know how you feel about the job and whether it's right for you. A probationary period for a new job is usually about three months. If you decide the new role isn't right for you, you can use the last month or two of your probationary period to search for other work. This gives you enough time to make a smooth transition from one job to another.

When you start a new job, it helps to have an exit strategy in place. You can then leave if you need to and not feel trapped in that job if it doesn't work out.

5. CHANGE IT UP

Reflectors can excel at many things. Our openness makes us receptive, knowledgeable, adaptable and wise. We don't have to limit ourselves to being only one thing for the rest of our lives. We have a natural ability to tune into other people and the world around us, which makes us great healers. We can help heal people physically, mentally, emotionally, and spiritually.

When you feel compelled to change jobs, do it. Reflectors find great joy in tackling new things. If you can, rediscover yourself through the evolution of your career. We have the ability to be good at many different things. Why not give yourself the opportunity to sample as many diverse jobs as possible to find the type of work that suits you best? If nothing else, you'll learn a lot in the process and gather even more wisdom.

I've learned so many things about myself, life, and other people through having a diverse career. Working as an actor gave me great insight into the inner workings of people, their emotions, and myself. Working as a teacher taught me how to synthesise information into comprehensible chunks so it can be digested properly. It was also a very rewarding job. I learned so much from teaching other people.

Running adventure tours in South East Asia gave me perspective; perspective on life and perspective on the clear similarities of people around the world with the same basic desire for love and connection. I also learned how to truly be in the moment during this phase in my life and just 'be' every day.

Working in the corporate world taught me about organisational structures and how constricting these are to the people within them. I learned that human nature is the same both outside and inside the confines of the organisation and that many people conform to expected behaviours even when they don't necessarily believe in them.

Experiencing each one of these jobs has shaped who I am today. I've learned so much about myself and humanity. I've really allowed my openness as a Reflector to sample the many different ways of working and being in this world.

THE CHALLENGE OF
WORKING AFTER 40

*Do something today that your future
self will thank you for.*
- Sean Patrick Flanery

W E'VE ALREADY ESTABLISHED that Reflectors
don't have sustainable energy. We need lots of breaks,
rest, and alone time to function as healthy Reflectors. We can
have intense energy bursts for short periods of time, but we
can't keep going and going without reprieve. We can easily
burn out by the time we reach 40 if we haven't been living our
strategy.

While Reflectors can still be vibrant in our older years, we
have a much greater chance of burning out than our Generator
friends. This means that, after 40, we may be less capable of
doing some of the things we did easily in our younger years.
If we've pushed ourselves too hard in our youth, we may also
find that we burn ourselves out completely by this age and
have trouble sustaining a job.

We might be able to cope in physically demanding work
and long work hours when we are young, but this is usually

not sustainable as we age. If we become incapable of sustaining a job after 40, and we aren't financially secure, we can struggle to support ourselves.

We need to put a plan in place while we're young that sets up our future self for financial support and success.

Solution – Plan Ahead for Your Work Future

Apart from marrying into money or coming from a wealthy family, most of us will need to find a way to support ourselves during our lives. Given we usually can't sustain a traditional job, particularly after 40, we need to approach work with the long game in mind.

If you establish an income stream when you're young, you can aim to work less and earn more when you're older and have less energy. In our youth, we have a greater capacity to study and work without completely frying our circuits. We can utilise our youthful vitality and our ability to draw on the energy of the people around us to put things in place that will sustain us when we are older and less capable of doing this.

Take the time to consider what type of work you enjoy doing that will sustain you into the future. You may enjoy sport and have the required athletic talent, but it's unlikely you'll be capable of sustaining a career as an athlete forever. If you choose this path early on, it is vital that you set up some other means of support that you can draw on when your career as an athlete is over.

Be more measured in your approach to work. Ensure your work choices are healthy for you and are sustainable.

I have a very colourful work history. I've sampled many jobs to discover the type of work I enjoy and can sustain doing. I've also completed three degrees. These degrees, along with some certifications, have given me a greater variety of work options and opportunities. They've also allowed me to find work that pays well, so I can work less hours and still earn a good income. I am grateful that my younger self put the effort into completing these degrees, so I can reap the benefits now that I no longer have the same energy levels.

In my early 30s, I set myself up as a knowledge expert in a particular field. This allowed me to find work that paid well. I also gained a lot of experience working in this field. As my energy levels started to dwindle after 35, I became a consultant, which gave me more work flexibility.

A few years later, I began working as a contractor in the same field. This paid more and gave me even greater flexibility. As a contractor, I could choose contract durations that suited me. It also allowed me to take time off between contracts if I needed.

Eventually, when I realised my energy levels could no longer sustain myself working within a traditional schedule and structure, I began working for myself. I started working just two or three days a week depending on how I felt. By setting myself up as a knowledge expert in a specific field and making deliberate work choices, I was able to earn as much in these two to three days of work as I once earned working five days a week. My dedication, and the effort I put in when I was more energetically capable, paid off when I needed it most.

By cautiously accessing energy in our youth, we can set ourselves up through study and work to support ourselves in a way that doesn't energetically drain our limited resources when we are older. This also helps us have a happier and healthier lifestyle. When we access energy in our youth to pursue work and study options, we need to ensure we don't push ourselves to the point of burnout.

Take the time to study, work, plan, and do everything you can to build a solid foundation for your future. You will then reap the rewards of your youthful endeavours when you need it most. As long as you are wise and considered in the way you access and use energy during this time, you can sustain yourself when you are older and less energetically capable.

Today, there are many different study options available that can be tailored to suit your specific needs. If full-time study seems overwhelming, you can do it gradually as a part-time student. Online study options are also a great way to study in your own time and at your own pace.

Consider all the different work options that are available to you which can potentially provide you with a good income stream. These should eventually compensate you well enough that you can work less or have more flexibly when you're older and still earn you enough to survive and even prosper.

Creating a passive income is a great way to support your future self. Even working towards a career that gives you flexibility is a positive step towards supporting and setting your future self up for success. You may even find a way to get other people to support you and your work. You may show other people the value you add to the world as a Reflector and allow others to take care of you. This is a wonderful path to take. It also helps to have a backup plan in place if you pursue this path.

COACHING TIPS

—————————— ⊏⊐ ——————————

1. FIND WORK YOU ENJOY

Spend time considering the type of work you enjoy. You may need to sample a few different jobs first to determine what brings you the most joy and satisfaction. What are your strengths? What do you love doing? What comes easy and naturally to you? These are all good questions to ask yourself in pursuit of finding your right work.

Many Reflectors are healers and teachers. This is work that we naturally feel compelled to engage in since we can magnify all that is around us and mirror it back to others. This allows us to be wise observers with plenty of knowledge to share and draw on to help guide other people.

It may take you several lunar cycles to determine the type of work that feels best for you. Ask the universe what fulfilling work you should do and see what shows up. Allow yourself to explore the possibilities. Talk through your ideas with trusted advisors. Even look at your life purpose within your Human Design chart. This can provide some guidance on what you're here to give the world.

Do whatever you can to find work that is aligned to your needs. Find work that you enjoy and that plays into your natural strengths and talents. This lightens the energetic strain that work often has on us. Determining what you enjoy doesn't have to be overly specific.

For example, you may discover that you love to teach. You don't have to decide what sort of teacher you want to be at this point or even what you want to teach. Deciding that teaching is something you feel aligned with is enough to get started.

Reflectors can do almost anything for work. Work that Reflectors naturally lean towards is often people-related. Some examples include:

- Coaching
- Healing
- Writing
- Bodywork
- Communication
- Teaching
- Social sciences
- Hospitality
- Community
- Therapies
- Counselling

Whatever you do, make sure you love it, it will truly make a difference to how you experience life as a Reflector.

2. DETERMINE HOW TO GIVE YOURSELF A SUSTAINABLE FUTURE

Determine how you can attain a sustainable future as a Reflector through the type of work you enjoy doing. Ensure the work you choose will potentially have at least one of the following features to support you when you are less energetically capable in the future.

a) **Flexible work schedule.** This means you don't have to work in a traditional 9 to 5 job. You have flexibility in either when you work or how you work to suit your energetic needs.

For example, if you choose to work as a coach, this allows you to schedule coaching appointments at times that suit you.

b) **Balanced lifestyle.** Work that gives you a balanced lifestyle allows you to play to your natural rhythm with lots of time for rest and

For example, a fly-in fly-out job may involve a roster of working one week and then having two weeks off (not working).

c) **High-paying job.** This type of work should allow you to work less when needed but still earns you enough to support

For example, being a consultant allows you to work a couple of days a week at a high pay rate which, comparatively, is worth a whole week's salary in other jobs.

d) **Passive income.** Create something that generates a passive income and requires minimal effort from you in the long term. Any revenue stream that doesn't tax you energetically is a great means to supporting yourself.

For example, create an online store and sell products online, such as e-books.

There are plenty of other ways you can set yourself up, doing work that you enjoy, allowing you to rest, and working in a way that suits your energetic needs as you age.

3. CREATE YOUR ROADMAP TO A COMFORTABLE FUTURE

Once you've thought about the type of work you enjoy, and how it will give you a sustainable future, it's time to work out how to get there. You must have a realistic plan in place to ensure you can successfully achieve these goals.

This roadmap should include all the things you need to do to reach your desired work future. This includes any study you need to undertake to reach your goal, such as university degrees, certifications, and other types of training. You will also need to determine any work experience required to gain credibility and exposure within your chosen field.

Regardless of whether you need to study or not, determine what is required to reach your work goals. Then, create a roadmap that details how you intend to get there.

4. FOLLOW YOUR ROADMAP

Regularly check back in with yourself to ensure this path you've mapped out still feels right for you. Ensure you're following the roadmap and adapting it as necessary to suit your changing needs. While the destination is important, make sure you also enjoy the journey.

A NOTE ABOUT GOING TO UNIVERSITY

If you need to go to university to achieve this goal, don't rule it out. Many young Reflectors think there is no way they can sustain themselves through a university degree. Attaining a degree is completely possible with the right parameters in place.

The keys to successfully attending university as a Reflector are listed below.

A. Choose the right degree. Make sure your degree is not only something you enjoy but is also something that will support and sustain your energetic needs in the future.

For example, you may enjoy flying so you consider studying to be an airline pilot. They earn a good wage, and this job will probably allow you to work less when you're older. However, the level of stress and pressure that these pilots are under, the lack of routine sleep, and constant change in time zones may not be the ideal choice for your health as a Reflector. This doesn't completely rule this career path out. Just be sure to look into it further to ensure there is a way to work within this field that is sustainable for you.

B. Choose study options that work best for you. Most courses offer several subject delivery modes that you can choose from.

Online study options are usually the most flexible of all. If you work best alone at home and at your own pace, studying online may be the best study option for you. If you lack motivation and energy when you're alone and you need to bounce off the energy of other people, then studying face-to-face may be the best study mode for you. A good mixture of different study options is sometimes the most successful way to accommodate your varying energetic needs.

Attending a class once a week for a semester may feel right for you. Taking the same class over a two-day weekend intensive may better suit your needs. There are plenty of study options available and many different places you can study so look elsewhere if one university doesn't offer you the study options you require.

When you need an energetic boost to get work done, sit in a library or among a group of fellow students so you can draw on their sacral energy, assuming they're Generator types. You may work harder and faster with these people around.

Remember to pay attention to your need for rest. Whatever study mode you choose, ensure it doesn't burn you out.

C. **Take as long as you need to complete the degree**. Don't put expectations on yourself to finish your degree in a specific time or try to keep up with everyone else. Set yourself realistic timeframes that you can change if you need to. You can study full-time or part-time. You can study for a year and then take a year off if you need. Work out the healthiest way for you to complete the degree. If you push yourself too hard to complete it too quickly, you may burn yourself out and not finish it at all.

By the time I started my master's degree, I didn't want to study for much longer. I knew how I studied most effectively, and I wanted to get through it as quickly as I could without burning myself out. Instead of taking two years to complete the degree, I finished it in one and a half years. I completed six subjects for two of the semesters so I could shave six months off the degree. This was a measured approach. I determined which subjects I could study together so I could complete more work at one time. Each semester was bookended with a break where I did absolutely nothing to allow myself to recover from the workload during the semester. This approach worked best for me.

PART FIVE

Deal With Pressure

REFLECTORS DON'T DO WELL under pressure. Our sensitive immune system and lack of sustainable energy means we easily crumble under the force of life pressures. We need to ensure that we don't succumb to these pressures and find ways to cope when the pressure is on.

Reflectors are designed to move slowly. We need to take our time, especially when making decisions. We are here to go with the flow rather than move swiftly through life, constantly doing. When we don't learn to deal with the pressure to act and decide quickly, against our natural disposition, we often end up physically, mentally, and emotionally drained. When we are drained, we can't function as vibrant, wise observers fulfilling our role in the world.

This section has four main challenges:

- Pressure to make decisions
- Pressure to do
- Mental pressure
- Pressure to speak

Each chapter within this section is dedicated to exploring one of these challenges and provides tips for effectively managing these pressures.

THE PRESSURE TO
MAKE DECISIONS

*You know you've made the right decision when there
is peace in your heart and freedom in your soul.*
                                                    - Unknown

UNLIKE GENERATOR TYPES, Reflectors can't ask yes
or no questions and feel a response in our gut every time
we need to make a big decision. Nor do we have an emotional
wave to help us feel what is right for us using our emotional
Solar Plexus centre.

A Reflectors' decision-making strategy is to wait through
a full lunar cycle before making a big decision. That's a long
28.5 days. A full lunar cycle is how long it takes for the moon
to move through and activate all 64 hexagram gates within the
Human Design body chart. When the gates at both ends of a
channel within the body chart are activated, they activate the
whole channel. Reflectors don't have any activated channels.
We only have activated gates. When the moon activates a gate
on the opposite side of the channel to one of our activated gates,

we are impacted and influenced by this activation because it gives us temporary definition in our chart.

For those eight hours or so when the moon activates one of these opposing gates, we experience the consistent energy of this whole channel and its connected energy centres. This can help with our decision-making process. When our Sacral centre is temporarily defined by this moon activation, we may experience a response in our gut. When our Ajna centre is temporarily defined, we may have certainty and clarity about our response. Taking a full lunar cycle to make a decision allows us to tune into the effect of these moon activations to help make a decision that feels right for us.

Taking this long to decide can be almost impossible in today's fast-paced world when decisions are often demanded in the moment. When we're offered a new job, we typically can't turn around and say, "I'll let you know in a month." When a flight goes on sale, we have to make a decision then and there otherwise we miss the opportunity. Allowing ourselves the full 28.5 days feels more like a luxury than a reality for most of our decisions.

Decision making is hard for Reflectors. Making quick decisions isn't natural for us. When we need to make decisions in the moment, we feel an undue amount of pressure and stress. The bigger the decision required, the more pressure we feel. We can feel under tremendous pressure to work out what feels right for us without ever truly sensing whether we've made the right decision or not. When we have to make quick decisions, we take a stab in the dark about what is right for us. We often make bad decisions for this very reason.

Reflectors often feel the implications of a big decision. We know that, if we get it wrong, it can have huge consequences on how we feel and on our life.

When I am pressured to make a big 'on-the-spot' decision, I literally feel sick. I freeze and my brain empties. I am also very aware of the broader implications these decisions have on my life. A while ago, my husband and I decided to renovate our house. We decided that the house should be repainted. One day we were out shopping and we ended up in a paint shop. He was discussing paint with the shop manager and suddenly they were both staring at me holding three different coloured buckets of paint asking me to choose one.

I froze. My brain literally couldn't process. I didn't mind any of the colours, but I had no idea which one would look best on the house. Paint colour looks much different on a house then it does on the side of a paint bucket.

While the decision was seemingly small in the scheme of life, it felt huge to me. I would be looking at the colour of my house for years to come. My home is my sanctuary. I need to feel good there. If I chose the wrong colour, I'd have to look at that bad decision every day. I was acutely aware that we couldn't just repaint the house if I made the wrong decision.

My husband is a Generator. He was able to use his gut instinct to choose these three colour options. I had no such internal indicator. I couldn't handle the pressure and, overwhelmed, I left the shop.

Even when we have the luxury of taking a full lunar cycle to make a decision, we still need strategies in place to help us make the right decision. We need a way to tap into ourselves and feel a decision in our body because we don't have a clear and consistent way of internally feeling what is right for us.

SOLUTION – TALK TO YOUR DECISION-MAKING CREW

When you have a big decision to make, give yourself as much time as possible to make the decision, ideally at least 28.5 days, or one full lunar cycle. When you have a full lunar cycle to make a decision, you can track the influence of the moon transits through each gate as they give you temporary definition in your chart. These activations will affect you in a consistent way across the lunar cycle and you can use them to feel out your right decision.

Do what you can to buy yourself as much time as you need when you have a decision to make. Don't be pressured into making a decision on the spot if you can avoid it. It's important that we aren't rushed into making decisions. Life becomes difficult when we're forced to make a decision without having the time needed to sense what is right for us.

If someone is putting pressure on you to make a decision, don't accept their timeframe unless these constrictive limitations are set. You might not be able to ask for more time when deciding about a new job, but you can definitely say to a friend you need more time to decide if you'll go away with her on vacation.

When faced with a big decision, Reflectors must find a way to make a decision during the time we have available. Regardless of how long we have to make a decision, we need strategies in place that help us feel out what is right for us during that time.

Talking to people is one of the most effective techniques Reflectors can use to make decisions. Talking out loud to the right people brings clarity about what is right for us. To use this technique effectively, we need a small group of people in our lives we can talk to about our decisions. These people must feel good to be around. We must respect them and their advice. We must feel comfortable enough to be honest and completely ourselves around them.

You can probably identify these people already. They will not only be good listeners, but they will allow you to talk candidly and will try not to interrupt you when you're sharing something important with them. They are the type of people who offer sound advice even if you don't take it. These people are a crucial aspect of your decision-making process. Note the friends, family, and colleagues who are already great listeners who can officially become part of your decision-making crew. These people make a great sounding board for you to talk to about upcoming decisions.

If you don't have anyone like this in your life, it's time to start looking for them. Ideally, you want to include people in your crew who know you, who truly listen to what you have to say, who see you for who you are, and who offer advice only when asked. It's important as a Reflector to have at least one person in your life that you can share your thoughts and decision-making process with.

Not everyone you love and care about will be suited to your decision-making crew. They need to be good listeners who allow you to talk so you can hear how you feel about your decision while you're talking about it.

My husband is an amazing man and there are many things I share with him. However, when I need to make an important decision, he is not one of my go-to people for decision-making help. This is because, as a man, he often wants to fix things. He's already thinking of solutions before I've even finished talking. His style isn't to sit back and listen deeply to what I have to share, so he doesn't always offer me advice that feels right for me. I also don't get the opportunity to talk uninterrupted, so I can hear what's right for me as I talk.

This crew of people may have something relevant and useful to share with you, or they may just be there to listen as your sounding board. Either way, talking to them when you have a decision to make is a great way to process a decision.

When faced with a big decision, you may also need to recruit temporary members to your decision-making crew. These are subject matter experts who can provide a specific perspective on a topic. If you have a decision to make about working for a different company, for example, it can help to talk through this decision with someone who has already worked there and who has experience in the subject you are making a decision about.

When I was deciding about whether to move to Dubai to live and work many years ago, I spoke to a couple of colleagues who once lived there. Their ears and advice helped shape my final decision. While my usual decision-making crew helped form my decision about moving, generally, these experts were able to give me subject matter advice and a perspective that wasn't available from the other members of my decision-making crew.

Sometimes, the advice from our crew really helps us. Other times, the process of talking openly and honestly with them allows us to hear and feel the right decision within ourselves. Just because our crew offers us advice about our decision, doesn't mean we have to take it. In fact, often their advice leads us to deciding the complete opposite. It's the process of talking it out and tuning into what aligns within us that is important. Whatever their advice, this process can really help Reflectors make better decisions.

Coaching Tips

1. WAIT A LUNAR CYCLE TO MAKE A DECISION – IF YOU CAN

As soon as you have a big decision to make, track how you feel about your decision during the next 28.5 days as the moon transits across the lunar cycle.

Use your temporary definition from these transits to feel a response to your decision in your body. Do you have a clear gut instinct when your Sacral centre is defined? Do you have certainty and clarity when your Ajna centre is temporarily defined? What about intuition in the Spleen when it is defined? Notice how you feel about the decision across all of your temporary activations.

If your decision remains consistent across the cycle, you can rely on making that choice. If not, you may need more time to decide, or it may not be the right time to make a decision.

2. SELECT YOUR DECISION-MAKING CREW

a) Make a list of the people you talk to and go to for advice. Ask yourself:

- Are they good listeners?
- Do they allow you to be yourself and allow you to be open and honest?
- Do you feel good around them?

If the answer is yes to all three of these questions, these people can be included in your decision-making crew.

b) Determine if there is anyone else in your life you could include in your crew who fit the above criteria.

c) Determine which members of your crew are best placed to help with particular decisions. You may have someone in your crew who is great to talk to about work decisions, another about family decisions, and yet another about travel decisions. You don't need to talk to every member of your crew for each decision you make. Sometimes talking to one person will suffice. Your crew should include a range of people that fulfil the above criteria who you can appropriately select and talk to when you have a big decision to make.

d) Enroll subject matter experts when required. These people will provide you with detailed knowledge and experience on a specific topic and will give you greater insight into the aspects of a particular decision you need to make. You will only need to engage these people to your crew while you are making a very specific decision.

3. TALK THROUGH YOUR DECISION WITH YOUR CREW

For each big decision you make, determine which members of your crew are best placed to help with this particular decision. Then, schedule in time to discuss it with them.

Let these people know that you need their support by being a sounding board for a decision you have to make. If you want them to also provide their thoughts and advice, ask for it. Let them know their input will be greatly received in helping you make an informed decision.

Take the time to listen to their thoughts and advice about the subject if you've asked for it. Notice how you feel when they share this with you. Become self-aware of what comes up for you when you are sharing information with your crew and when they are offering you feedback or advice. This self-awareness will help you determine how you truly feel about the decision and what is right for you regardless of what is discussed.

If all else fails and you don't have anyone else to talk through your decision with, talk out loud to yourself. Just hearing the words leave your mouth can help in knowing what is right for you.

4. MAKE A DECISION

Talking through your decision with your crew should help lead to a decision that feels right for you, regardless of how long you have to make the decision. Even if this decision goes against what everyone else advises, if it feels right for you after this process, stick with your decision.

You should ultimately feel the right decision somewhere within your body. Your body will communicate what is correct for you. Don't listen to what's in your mind or make a decision in your head. Don't overthink it. You will feel something in your gut, within your body, or you will intuitively hear it as you speak. Be observant and let yourself feel what is right for you. This will be your answer.

THE PRESSURE TO DO

It's not the load that breaks you, it's the way you carry it.
- Lou Holtz

WHEN THE ROOT CENTRE is defined, people experience an adrenaline pulse that is either on or off. When the pulse is on, they have the energy to do something. When the pulse is off, they no longer have the energy to do it and they can happily stop whatever they are doing and rest. Reflectors have this centre open. We don't have this same internal on/off adrenaline pulse. When something needs to be done, we feel pressure to get it done as soon as possible. We don't have an off switch that signals to us when it's time to stop and rest.

My husband has a defined Root centre. On the weekends, he likes to do chores in the yard. When he is ready, and only when he's ready, he goes into the yard and starts these chores. In the meantime, I'm inside madly doing the household chores. I go as fast as I can to get them done so I can be free of them. Meanwhile, my husband is happily pottering around in the garden getting things done like he has all the time in the world.

Often, I will pop my head out during my mad flurry of chores to ask him a question only to find he is no longer in the yard but instead in bed having a nap. The lawn may be half mowed or the trees may be half pruned but his adrenaline pulse is off, so he's taking a break. Meanwhile, I'm stressed to the eyeballs washing and mopping floors trying to get it all done so I can be free of the chores. More than five minutes of downtime is enough to cause me to get straight back to it. I can't relax properly until it's all complete. This is the difference between having an open Root centre and having a defined Root centre.

An open Root centre causes Reflectors to have long lists of things to do, which we attempt to finish so we can be free. The only problem is that this to-do list is rarely ever complete. Things are added to the list as quickly as they are crossed off it, and it becomes a never-ending list of tasks. We feel constant pressure to get these things done so we can be free of these tasks. This makes it hard for us to relax for long. We have an inner nagging telling us to get things done. This is an exhausting way to live.

We also pick up on this adrenaline pulse energy from people with a defined Root centre and amplify it. We feel this adrenaline pressure even when someone isn't actually applying this pressure on us - we feel pressure from them energetically. This causes us to add more things to our to-do list and, consequently, causes us a lot more stress.

When we continue to push and use adrenaline energy to achieve things while under stress, we lead ourselves down a very unhealthy path. Our open Root centre makes us susceptible to pressure within ourselves and from the people around us to get things done.

If we don't learn to stay out of this pressure and stop pushing ourselves with energy we don't have, we will eventually burn out, become chronically ill, and even struggle getting back to a normal life with a reasonable amount of stress.

SOLUTION – STOP TRYING TO GET IT ALL DONE

Awareness is the key to working with our open Root centre. This centre will always cause us to have a long list of things to do. When we realise how this centre affects us, we can stop trying to get it all done. We can be more selective about what we put on our to-do list and ensure that we set ourselves realistic timeframes to achieve these tasks. We can also use this information to learn to say no to tasks whenever we can and offload tasks to other people. The important thing is that we don't take on so much that we fry our circuits.

Notice when you feel under the most pressure. Notice if you're around someone with a defined Root centre. While you're in this person's presence you may continue to absorb and amplify this adrenaline energy and feel their pressure even when they haven't said anything.

Many years ago, I borrowed money from a flat mate. We agreed that I would pay the money back once I'd finished studying and was in full-time work. A short while later, while I was still studying, I took a part-time job. My flat mate was trying to save for an overseas trip at this time. Although she never said anything to me about the money, I felt pressure to pay her back as soon as possible now that I was earning money and she needed funds for her trip.

I took on extra hours at work, stressing myself out while also juggling university, so I could save and pay her back as quickly as possible. When I gave her the money, she was shocked. She had no expectation of receiving it until much later. While she was trying hard to save for her trip, she never once considered the money I owed her to be repaid in time for her travels. I acted upon the pressure I felt from her defined Root centre, which was pressure to save money, but which wasn't at all directed at me.

The lesson here is to listen to what people say about pressure-based topics rather than reacting to the pressure you feel from them. Don't get sucked into the pressure you've picked up from their defined Root centre. If you're not sure if the pressure is real, ask them. You'll be surprised how often you have mistaken their Root centre pressure for actual pressure directed at you.

By noticing this, you have the power to consciously stop giving into the pressure. You can work out what is achievable and stop trying to get it all done. Remove yourself from people with defined Root centres for a while if this helps. Most importantly, determine what pressure is real and then work out what you can realistically achieve in a day, a week, or a month and set yourself realistic goals.

When you need to, ask yourself, "what's the worst thing that will happen if I don't finish or achieve this?" Most of the time, the answer is nothing significant, so lighten the pressure load from yourself.

COACHING TIPS

1. WRITE A TO-DO LIST

Writing a to-do list is a cathartic process when you have a long list of action items running through your head. It helps alleviate the pressure of remembering all the things you need to achieve. It's a good way to capture these activities so you can stop thinking about them and start doing them. You can then cross them off your list and finally remove the pressure of each task.

2. HIDE YOUR TO-DO LIST

While it may be a useful process to write things down in a list, don't hold yourself to account trying to get them all done. Staring at a long list of action items can often add to your stress levels. Seeing all those items that need to be done, often within time constraints, can be completely overwhelming.

It's useful to capture these items into a list so they are out of your head, but don't keep them in a place where you'll continually see them. Look at your list, determine the top two or three items that you can realistically achieve that day or that week, and then hide the to-do list so that it's out of sight. If you need to add to the to-do list, pull it out, write the extra items on the list, and then hide it again out of sight.

When you've achieved those two or three initial items, revisit the list. When you are ready, choose the next two or three items. Then repeat the process. This allows you to feel like you're progressing, but it removes the pressure to do it all at once. This also removes the stress of continually looking at a long list of items that you may never complete.

3. STOP TRYING TO GET IT ALL DONE

This pressure to constantly get things done comes from within us. We are the ones who usually put these expectations on ourselves due to our open Root centre. Often this pressure is unwarranted. Therefore, only we can control within ourselves this pressure to constantly get things done.

If we had all the energy and time in the world, we could achieve many things. The reality is we don't. Even Generators can feel this pressure if they have an open Root centre. However, as a Reflector without a motor centre, when we push ourselves beyond our limits, we can do ourselves serious harm.

It is vital that we stop trying to get it all done. We will never get everything done because our list will keep on growing. We need to learn to live with the pressure of the Root centre.

Ask yourself what tasks are important and really matter to you. If you can, ask someone else to help. Then get rid of the other tasks or just let them go.

You'll be surprised at how many things don't actually matter if they never get done. The key here is to be realistic with your goals and ensure they align with what you are physically and mentally capable of doing. This means that sometimes you need to give up completing a task so you can focus on another.

When I'm in my flow of writing, I have to let go of trying to keep a clean and tidy house. I focus on the essential tasks, like eating, and ensure I'm living in reasonably sanitized conditions, but jobs like polishing the silver, dusting, and mopping the floor are kept well off the list.

4. CHECK IN WITH YOURSELF WHEN YOU FEEL UNDER PRESSURE

When you feel under pressure, check in with yourself to understand why. Are you around other people who are unconsciously putting pressure on you through their defined Root centre? Is someone actually putting pressure on you to achieve something? Identify where the pressure is coming from and deal with it. If it's due to someone else's adrenaline energy, remove yourself from them for a while to let the pressure subside.

When you feel your heart rate pumping and anxiety pressure setting in, stop what you are doing and take stock. Do whatever you can to recognise the source of the pressure and find immediate ways to alleviate it. Nothing is worth getting sick over.

5. ALLEVIATE THE PRESSURE

When you feel adrenaline pressure and anxiety starts to consume you, find ways to offload this pressure. Find a technique for reducing stress and pressure that works for you.

There are many different options. Some people reduce their pressure by sitting in silence, other people like the distraction of noise to drown out their active doing thoughts. How you remove this pressure isn't important. What's important is that you find a way to take the pressure off yourself.

Some ways to alleviate the pressure of the Root centre are listed below.

- Focus on achieving only one or two things at a time.
- Set yourself realistic timeframes to complete tasks.

- Lower your expectations about how much you will achieve
- Offload tasks to other people
- Take lots of breaks when completing tasks, so you have a balance between doing and rest time

Remember, Reflectors are here to go with the flow. We are here to BE, not DO. Don't get caught up trying to do too much at any one time - leave that to the Manifesting Generators who are designed to multi-task. We can't fulfil our need to BE when we are busy doing. Reevaluate your life. Is it time you made some changes to the way you're existing and how much you're trying to get done?

THE PRESSURE
OF THE MIND

*Sometimes the worst place you can
be is inside your own head.*

\- Nabil Memon

THE HEAD IS THE CENTRE for ideas and inspiration.
Reflectors have this centre open which means we don't
have consistency in this centre. We experience many different
ways of receiving ideas and inspiration, which can overwhelm
us.

Our open Head centre constantly absorbs the ideas and
inspirations of people around us with defined Heads. We
download their ideas without knowing that they aren't meant
for us. We wonder what to do with them, why we received
them, and how we can implement them. Our minds can be
in a constant spin of confusion, doubt, and suspicion. This
continous stream of inspiration makes for a very busy Reflector
mind. Not only are we inundated with ideas, we also feel
compelled to process them. This is why the Head is also called
a pressure centre. We feel under pressure to figure things out
or turn them into actions.

I often lie awake at night unable to sleep because I get a download of thoughts. Sometimes, these are thoughts about things I forgot to do during the day. Sometimes, these are ideas about something I could do. Other times, these thoughts are just ponderings about life or what has happened during the day. I often wake in the night because a random thought pops into my head. The other night, I woke in the early hours thinking about buying a bread maker. I don't eat a lot of bread, but there this thought was keeping me up at night.

These ideas can consume us. Then, just like that, they can slip away. Our open Head also causes us to pick up on other people's ideas. Without realizing it, we can suddenly be chasing a thought about something that isn't even for us. When this person leaves our company, the idea can disappear with them. Sometimes, we try to hang onto the idea believing it's ours to be actioned. We can spend a lot of our time consumed with ideas absorbed from other people, not realizing they were never ours in the first place.

Ten years ago, I got caught up in a huge idea to start a unique event business. I met a woman at a barbeque, and we found ourselves in similar life circumstances: in our thirties, single, and childless. She couldn't have children, and I was still hoping for them but had been very unlucky in love. She was sick and tired of always being the only female at these occasions without children. She was also frustrated that most of the female conversations at these events revolved around dirty nappies and other child-rearing topics. An idea leaped into my head and then bounced out of my mouth about starting our own events business for "adult-only childfree events." And, thus, a business was born.

This was her dream and passion. I loved the idea while around her and worked hard at breathing life into it. We met often to turn the idea into a reality and put labour, money, and love into it. The idea took off. We had interest in the business nationally. We were on morning talk shows and other national TV shows. I even had a double-page-spread article about me in the city newspaper.

It was a great idea. It obviously had legs. But, I hadn't entered it correctly. I didn't stop to consider if this was my idea, my passion, or my drive that I was following. I was good at running events and promoting things, but the actual purpose behind it was not something I'd spent much time considering – and, I definitely didn't take 28.5 days to think about it.

One day at an event, a woman said to me that she believed I was leading something big. Like the burning of the bras movement in history, she said I had started something revolutionary to help women without children feel more socially accepted and less judged. I liked the idea, but was it mine? Did I really want to be the face of this?

In the midst of this, I found out that, if I wanted children of my own, my only option was to go through IVF immediately. So here I was, in the middle of being the voice and frontwoman of a childfree revolution, secretly jabbing myself with needles every day in hope that I would not end up childfree myself.

A month or so later, when a prime-time current affairs television program contacted me to do an interview on their show as the literal voice of childfree women, I finally realized that I had been chasing someone else's dream. I was completely in support of what these women wanted, but it was not my story. It wasn't my passion or my idea. After a year of hard work and a lot of money, we decided to close down the event company that wasn't mine to pursue in the first place.

With mental pressure comes stress. When we feel pressure to solve the what, why, and how questions for the ideas that constantly bombard us, it can be hard to sleep at night or find time to truly relax our mind. We can be filled with confusion and doubt. All of this overthinking usually taxes our already limited energy reserves.

SOLUTION – GET OUT OF YOUR HEAD

Reflectors must let go of the pursuit to find answers and solutions to the ideas and questions that dance through our minds. We should enjoy the flow of ideas and inspirations that come in and out of our heads but try not to hold on too tight to any of them. When we use our mind to wonder, it can be an amazing tool that lets us engage with all the different possibilities of thinking. It helps us fulfil our role in becoming truly wise, because we allow ourselves to enjoy a plethora of possibilities and we can see many different perspectives.

When ideas pop into your head, enjoy them if they feel good. If the ideas aren't pleasant, acknowledge them and then let them fall away. Reflectors are here to sample these things, and we should allow them to flow through us but not stick to us.

If you want certainty or clarity about an idea you can't let go of, turn the idea into a question. Speak out loud or in your head to the universe with a question about your idea. For example, ask, "Should I begin making quilt covers for the nursing home around the corner?" Instead of dwelling on the idea and overthinking it, ask a question about it and see what shows up in your life. Give yourself time to sense whether this is an idea that is yours and whether you should take action. Your response will never come to you in your head by overthinking it. It will show up in other ways within you or externally. Use your head to ask questions about your ideas and then let them go. Letting go can be hard for Reflectors, but it is essential for living a healthy and manageable life. This centre is for dreaming, not for doing.

When you find yourself overthinking or feeling stressed by all the noise in your head, find a way to relax or distract your mind. The activity to relax must get you out of your head. Some people can do this by meditating. Others don't find meditating distracting enough for their mind to relax. Other activities to get out of your head include exercising, reading, or even having a glass of wine. Find a strategy that helps remove the stress of your overactive, busy mind. This is vital so you don't burn yourself out mentally.

I have a couple of strategies that help me personally. I like to listen to inspiring podcasts while I walk on the beach. The salt air and extra oxygen I receive physically relaxes me. The podcasts get me into a different frame of mind and shift my thinking to a more relaxed state. Sometimes, when my brain is overactive at night and walking isn't an option, I like to sit on my deck with a glass of wine and look out at my yard. Other times, it helps me to rest my mind for a couple of hours by watching a movie that really engages me mentally, so I'm exported into the storyline of the film. Other times, playing with my young nephews distracts me completely from the busyness of my mind because I am only focused on the 'now' while with the children.

Whatever you have to do to give you mind a break from the overwhelming pressure of thinking and figuring things out, start doing it now.

COACHING TIPS

1. DON'T TRY TO FIND ANSWERS

Whenever you receive an idea or an inspiration, don't automatically seek answers or actions for it. Merely notice the thought, bask in the idea if it feels good to do so, and then let it go. If you want an answer to this inspiration, ask a question out loud to the universe and then let it go. Don't think on it much more than that. Instead, wait and see what shows up in your world or within yourself in response to the question you asked and act accordingly.

2. FIND WAYS TO GET OUT OF YOUR HEAD

There are many different strategies you can use to get out of your head when you are caught in overthinking. When the mental chatter is pressuring you to find answers and take actions, choose a strategy that works for you to remove this pressure.

When you find yourself consumed with mental pressure, try one of the strategies below to get out of your head:

- Meditate
- Go for a walk
- Listen to music
- Listen to a podcast
- Watch a movie
- Go out with friends
- Take a nap
- Read a book
- Dance

- Play a sport
- Have a glass of wine or beer

The intention here is to redirect your thoughts so you remove and reduce the stress of mental pressure on your mind and ultimately reduce the likelihood of burning yourself out.

When you find yourself awake at night because your mind is in overdrive, find a way to download the ideas and get them out of your head, so you can relax and go to sleep. Keeping a journal and pen next to the bed can be a good way of getting the ideas out of your head. Another technique is to use your phone to record your ideas vocally.

When an idea pops into your head, notice it. Notice where it may have come from. Notice if this is something that feels right for you to do something with. The more you notice, the more you'll recognise when an idea is plaguing your mind so you can then take measures to control it.

3. LEARN TO BASK IN POSSIBILITIES

When you let go of your need for action and answer all the ideas and inspirations that come into your head, you have the potential to enjoy the wonder of possibility thinking. You can let the ideas pass through your mind without the need to do something with them.

When you stop trying to find answers and responses to the ideas and questions in your mind, you allow yourself to bask in these ideas. Have fun with them and expand your wisdom about what is possible.

THE PRESSURE TO SPEAK

*Wisdom is the reward you get for a lifetime of
listening when you'd have preferred to talk.*
- Doug Larson

REFLECTORS HAVE AN OPEN Throat centre. This is
the centre for communication and manifestation. People
who have this centre defined and also have a connected motor
centre (Manifestors and Manifesting Generator types), They
can initiate conversations and certain actions. Their voice
instills confidence in others and people tend to listen to them
when they speak. They have the ability to turn words into
actions.

Reflectors have a hard time converting words into actions
because of our open Throat centre. When we speak without
waiting for the right time to share, we spend a lot of energy
trying to get people's attention so we can be heard. We also
run the risk of our words not being heard as intended, which
feels like no one is listening. The pressure we put on ourselves
to be noticed can cause us to push with our voice and raise it
in an attempt to get people to listen. It can also cause us to talk
too much. When we have something important to say, we can
become extremely disappointed when no one is listening.

For these reasons, we often feel invisible. We struggle to get the recognition and the attention we need. We may even take inappropriate actions to get recognition, which usually doesn't give us the right type of attention.

At school, I had a teacher who didn't particularly like me. I'm not exactly sure why, but I often felt ignored and neglected in her class. It was a music class and most of the other students were musically gifted. I loved music and singing, but I wasn't an auditory learner. I only played instruments using sheet music. In that classroom, I developed a class-clown persona. I would do all sorts of silly things that would get the attention of my classmates and the teacher. Naturally, it didn't make her like me more, but I no longer felt ignored.

When we speak and no one hears us or our words aren't received as intended, we are often compelled to talk more and to project our voices louder as a way to demand that others listen. We become loud, over-talkative, and noisy in our quest to be heard. Our open Throat centre can cause us to blurt things out without knowing exactly what we're going to say, often without first listening properly to the other person. This can also make us interrupters and overtalkers. But, this strategy only worsens the problem. We may have something important to say, but when we talk without being invited to share, our wisdom falls upon mostly deaf ears.

When Reflectors can't communicate in a way that is heard, we can't share our wisdom with our community and the world. Reflectors must learn to harness the power of the open Throat and work with its limitations, so we can ultimately fulfil our roles as wise observers with oodles of wisdom to share.

Solution – Talk Less, Listen More

With an open Throat centre, Reflectors are designed for silence. When we wait in silence, our aura does the talking. People are drawn to us and want to hear what we have to say. If we want to be heard and we want our words to have impact, we must wait for an invitation to speak.

You don't necessarily have to wait for a formal invitation, but rather, it's about waiting for the right timing when other people are receptive to what you have to say. Someone may ask you for your opinion. You may feel the conversation going in a particular direction, leading to an opening for you to share your words appropriately. If someone engages you as a coach, this is their invitation for you to communicate with them. Essentially, waiting for an invitation means you aren't pushing your words out there onto other people. When you push, no one hears you properly. Worse still, they may find you obnoxious and rude.

We must heed the fact that we have one mouth for talking and two ears for listening. We must listen before we speak. By listening in silence, we also hear more. We can tune in more to what is and is not being said by others. This grows our wisdom. When we do speak, our words have greater impact.

When you have something important to say, other people will pick this up in your aura while you're sitting there silently listening. People may then ask for your advice or your opinion. When you are recognised and called out to speak in this way, you get access to the energy of the Throat centre, which ensures other people listen to what you have to say.

If you don't believe me - try it. Sit quietly when engaged in conversation with a group of people and notice how people begin to recognise when you have something important to say.

In a previous job, I attended regular meetings about a project I was working on as a subject matter expert. When I first attended those meetings, I had an agenda of things I wanted to say only to find no one really listened to my advice, and I struggled to deliver my message. I pushed with my voice trying to get a word in among the many other people in the meeting.

After a while, I changed tactics. I attended these meeting with no set agenda. I just sat back and listened. When I started listening, I began to hear what was really going on. There were some underlying political agendas for some people in the meeting and this was causing the meetings to rarely finish with clear outcomes. When I began listening in silence, I noticed that someone would always turn to me and ask for my input and opinion. When I spoke on these occasions, people listened more intently. My words had greater impact and the meetings began to have better outcomes.

Naturally, this doesn't mean you can't ever speak first. There will be plenty of times you need to speak without being asked. But, when you have something important to contribute, or you want people to really hear what you have to say, practice silently listening until you are called out to speak, or wait for the right timing to deliver your words when others are ready to hear them.

One of the gifts of having an open Throat centre is that we absorb the communication and manifestation energy of people with a defined Throat. We then express this energy out in a way that best meets the needs of the people we are communicating with. This means we can adjust what we say and how we say it, so that our messages have maximum impact. When we use this energy properly, we become effective communicators, delivering important messages of wisdom.

COACHING TIPS

1. TRULY LISTEN

Sit silently and listen to other people whenever you can. When you do this, you really hear what people are saying and what they are not saying. Listening gives you wisdom. Listening also allows you to focus on the communication needs of the other person. When you do speak, you can adapt your voice and words appropriately to match theirs for maximum impact.

2. WAIT FOR AN INVITATION TO SPEAK

Stop talking because of your internal pressure to be heard and recognised. Instead, sit silently and listen. When you sit silently listening, your aura does the talking. Others will recognise that you have something important to say, and they will invite you to speak. When you do finally speak after being invited, your words will be truly heard by others. You will more effectively deliver your message and attain the recognition and attention you desire.

Summary

The Key To Living A Happy
And Healthy Reflector Life

REFLECTORS HAVE AN IMPORTANT role to play in the world. We are not designed to be like everyone else. When Reflectors live authentically and as designed, we can become the wisest and most objective people on the planet. The world needs our assistance. We can help move humanity forward. We can reflect back to the world the injustices that humanity inflicts upon itself. We must do this to be the mirror the world needs.

We are tough. We are the only Human Design type with the ability to sample the energies of the people around us and, using our resistant Teflon aura, not let them condition us. We are the one percenters. We can get a true sense of things without being burdened by them.

We see great hope in the world, because we feel the true nature of all living things beneath their conditioning. For this reason, even in a capitalist society where most of the population has forgotten the true value of life and how to live authentically, we can see the beauty and potential of humanity.

You must step up into your design and not be afraid of it. You mustn't be at the mercy of conditioning through your open centres, but rather use your openness to gain wisdom about every aspect of life. When you harness your aura's natural Teflon ability, you can sample energy without letting it consume you.

You must look after your health and stop pushing yourself with borrowed energy. Slow down and go with the flow as much as you can. You can't do your job if you're sick and burnt out. Remove expectations about how much you can physically do and achieve. You will achieve more by being still and silent and letting the right opportunities come to you.

Don't overthink things. Give yourself the time and space you need to be in the moment so you can observe the world. You can't observe the world properly while you are actively participating in it and 'doing' all the time.

Notice yourself. When words blurt out of your mouth or you feel an emotional ping, note where that came from. Become self-aware so you can not only understand yourself, but you can release what is not your own and what is not serving you.

Choose your friends and relationships carefully. Make sure the people you reflect the most give you healthy reflections. You will often become these people so ensure they are truly happy and healthy individuals. Don't just fall for their potential.

When you give up trying to force things and allow yourself to go with the flow, you demonstrate trust in the universe. The more you trust and live in the moment, the more the right opportunities find you and you can be your authentic self.

This book has discussed the most important things Reflectors can do to live a happy and healthy life. As a Reflector you must:

- Know yourself
- Connect with people

- Keep healthy
- Find sustainable work
- Deal with pressure

In summary, the way to mitigate these Reflector challenges and live a healthy and happy Reflector life is to:

- Protect yourself
- Discharge your conditioning
- Find your right place and right people
- Explore for perspective
- Tune into your intuition
- Understand your energy needs
- Manage your time
- Rest, restore, and rejuvenate
- Get a good night's sleep
- Pay attention to your health
- Remove and protect yourself from people's energy
- Choose your partner wisely
- Balance your time spent alone and with others
- Find a sustainable way to work
- Plan ahead for your work future
- Talk to your decision-making crew
- Stop trying to get it all done
- Get out of your head
- Talk less, listen more

Once you fully step into your role as a Reflector and understand how you are designed to be different, you have the ability to share what you know and benefit humanity in your own remarkable way.

Be authentic. Do you. Become wise. I dare you. Be the mirror the world needs. You may find that fully living your design as a Reflector is not only a beautiful gift to the world, but also an amazing journey to embark on.

May you fall madly in love with yourself.

ACKNOWLEDGEMENTS

MY THANKS GO TO MANY people who directly and indirectly made this book possible.

I have to start by thanking my gorgeous husband Scott who has been patient and tolerant of my dedication to the writing process and for his incredible support and encouragement that allowed me to write this book.

Thanks to everyone on the GracePoint Publishing team who bought this book to life. A special thanks to Michelle Vandepas for her encouragement and advice across the whole writing process. I feel blessed to work with a publisher and team who really put the 'soul' into soul business.

To my mentor and friend Karen Curry Parker for her eternal inspiration, for her care and dedication to the world of Human Design, and for all her support over my own human design educational journey.

To my friend Lisa Symons who introduced me to Human Design and who continues to inspire and encourage me to follow my dreams.

Acknowledgements

To my mother Valerie Allum, thank you for always believing in me. No matter what life has thrown at me she has continued to initiate me into new endeavours and been an amazing sounding board that's helped me so much on my own Reflector journey.

To all the Reflectors I have had the privilege of working with and helping on their Reflector journey, thank you for allowing me to grow and learn more about our type through our time together. It takes strength and trust to be open and vulnerable with an almost stranger. I am ever grateful for your honesty and openness during these sessions.

And finally, to my family; my mother, father, sister, brother and close friends. Thank you for bringing me up in an unconditionally loving and supportive environment. Thank you for trusting in me and allowing me to be me even when it seemed at odds with what you thought I should be doing. Thank you for being kind, caring, and nurturing souls who I had the fortune of reflecting back for most of my youth. I am entirely grateful for the life you have allowed and encouraged me to live as a Reflector.

ABOUT THE AUTHOR

Amber Clements is a rare Human Design Reflector. Born in England and raised in Australia, she grew up with adventurous parents seeking a better life. She is a transformation coach, professional facilitator, certified Human Design Specialist, qualified change manager, and has over 20 years of teaching experience. Amber holds a master's degree in communication and has a passion for education and creating simplicity from complexity. As an organisational change expert, she has spent the past decade helping individuals and organisations navigate their way through transitions and transformations.

Amber enjoys working with people from the inside out. She is available for private consultations, as a keynote speaker, and to conduct seminars and workshops.

You can reach her at

info@amberclements.com

or visit her online at
www.amberclements.com

For more great books please
visit HumanDesignPress.com

Made in the USA
Las Vegas, NV
21 October 2022

57849153R00129